Six Day War

Six Day War

A J Barker

Editor-in-Chief: Barrie Pitt
Editor: David Mason
Art Director: Sarah Kingham
Picture Editor: Robert Hunt
Consultant Art Editor: Denis Piper
Designer: David Allen
Illustration: John Batchelor
Photographic Research: Carina Dvorak
Cartographer: Richard Natkiel

Photographs for this book were especially selected from the following archives: Associated Press, London; Keystone, London; Camera Press, London; United Press International, London; Topix, London; Popperfoto, London; J, Arad, Israel; Central Press, London

First Printing: June 1974
Printed in United States of America

Ballantine Books
A division of Random House, Inc.
201 East 50th Street New York NY 10022

Contents

Mediterranean cockpit

Introduction by Barrie Pitt

The Six Day War did not bring Israel the peace which its founding fathers had hoped for. While this book was going to press the Middle East erupted again, and once more Arabs and Israelis were locked in a bloody conflict involving tens of thousands of troops and more tanks than were deployed at Stalingrad or Alamein during the Second World War.

The fighting started on Yom Kippur, the holiest and also the quietest day of the Jewish Year, when the whole of Israel had virtually shut down and many servicemen were home on leave. Under the cover of an intense artillery barrage and air bombardments, Egyptian troops surged across the Suez Canal and the Syrians simultaneously attacked the Israeli positions on the Golan Heights. Both Egypt and Syria have claimed that the Israelis provoked their invasion by firing on positions in Egypt and Syria. But the reports of UN observers have not confirmed any provocation; and the evidence clearly indicated that this fourth Arab-Israeli war in twenty-five years had been precipitated by the Arabs.

The fighting has not been a carbon copy of the Six Day War. This time the Israelis appear to have been caught off guard, and in the first few days of the war they paid a heavy price for their failure to launch a pre-emptive strike against the build-up of Arab forces. While Israel mobilized, her troops holding the Golan Heights and manning the Bar-Lev defences on the east bank of the Suez Canal were compelled to slog it out, taking heavy casualities – something which the Egyptians are better able to accept than the Israelis. As Israeli Intelligence knew that the Arabs were concentrating troops for an attack, it seems that the Israeli Government was prepared to take a military risk and allow its own forces to be attacked first rather than be accused of having started another war.

For two weeks the Arab armies forçed Israel to fight huge grinding battles which chewed up hundreds of tanks and thousands of men, and it quickly became evident that both the Egyptians and the Syrians had taken advantage of six years of training with vast quantities of modern Russian weapons. In these two weeks the role of the Israeli Air Force was drastically curtailed due to the effectiveness of the SAM missiles deployed in new integrated defence systems immediately behind the Suez Canal and below the Golan Heights. Only when these SAMs were knocked out by ground troops was the Israeli Air Force able to attain anything approaching the air superiority it enjoyed during the Six Day War.

Soviet-made anti-tank missiles are also reported to have taken a heavy toll of Israeli tanks. (An estimated 840 Israeli tanks were knocked out before the cease-fire came into effect, and most of these are said to have fallen to RPG-7 rocket-launched grenades or Sagger and Snapper anti-tank missiles.)

Early hopes of something less than a major war and expectations of another quick debacle for the Egyptians were shattered. Hopes that no dangerous strain would be thrown on the respective guarantors of Israel and the Arabs – the United States and the Soviet Union – also proved premature. In its third week the war reached a critical turning point, and the Israelis were within sight of a resounding clear-cut victory when both sides were pressured by their guarantors into accepting a cease-fire. In the course of the frenzied negotiations to arrange this cease-fire it appears that the two super-powers themselves came to the brink of nuclear war.

Israel's reluctance to stop fighting when she had regained the upper hand is understandable. She has had enough experience of United Nations and other guarantees and assurances to know what Czechoslovakia must have felt like in 1939. In a sense it was the United Nations which triggered off the Six Day War, and over the years the UN has tended to turn a blind eye to Arab attacks and an eagle eye on Israeli retaliations. Moreover Washington's priority now seems to be 'East-West detente', and the Arab oil threat to America, Europe and Japan will continue to be a powerful weapon in the continuing diplomatic and political battle. So, although the Israelis are not as innocent and reasonable as they sometimes like to make out, their basic fears are wholly understandable. In short Israel's sovereignity is limited by geography, history, size and population – and as long as the Russians and Arabs are in league with each other there can be no secure and viable borders for Israel without an external guarantee given and backed by the United States.

The huge quantities of modern weapons used and destroyed by both sides in this latest conflict demonstrate how totally dependent the Arabs and Israelis are for survival on the military aid provided by their sponsors. The Arabs have now demonstrated that with Soviet help they have gone a long way towards closing the technological gap which separates the Arab and Israeli military machines. They have also come to realize that they can never hope to beat the Israelis without the equipment which Russia supplies. And as there is no alternative source of supply, the Russian position in the Middle East can only get stronger. Meanwhile the Israelis must now fear that a day of reckoning is drawing steadily closer. Unless this war is followed by a negotiated peace settlement, it seems likely that there will be another explosion in the next few years. And next time an Israeli victory might prove even more elusive.

Ironically enough, Israel's failure to win this new war in the convincing style of 1967 may actually make it easier for her to achieve the goal she failed to attain after the Six Day War. Arab loss of face then made negotiations with the Israelis virtually impossible; following their defeat, the Arabs were convinced that talks could only result in the victor dictating terms to the vanquished. But the performance of Egyptian and Syrian troops in October 1973 has boosted Arab pride, and if the superpowers can bring the Arabs and Israelis together at the conference table, the latest conflict may bring Israel a kind of peace that victory in the Six Day War never brought. But if no settlement is forthcoming, and the Israelis have to face another crisis like that of June 1967 or October 1973, their country could become the site not of New Jerusalem but of Armageddon.

To the brink

In the short hot summer of 1967 the Arab-Israeli conflict which had festered for a generation exploded with abrupt and stunning violence which subsided almost before the shockwaves broke. It took just six days to redraw the map of the Middle East, as the forces of Israel quadrupled the size of their country in a campaign which was probably the most sensationally swift and complete ever recorded in the annals of war.

Yet this is one war which, if not inevitable, can hardly be judged to have been unexpected. The 'Middle East problem' has existed since time immemorial, and it will probably continue to do so, since it involves the most bitter and most intractable of passions, rooted in race, religion and riches. For nineteen years two million tough and resourceful Jews in the new State of Israel had lived in an atmosphere of tension and uncertainty, surrounded on three sides by 50 million Arabs. They had escaped the *shtetls* of Poland and Russia, overcome the holocaust of Nazi Germany, and had turned the deserts of Palestine into a market garden. But they were penned in by implacable enemies. From Beirut to the Atlas Mountains there lay a huge lake of hatred, which had overflowed twice before – in 1948 and 1956. Twice the Arabs had been defeated, but their defeats had only exacerbated their hatred of the 'Western abscess' in their midst. Divided among themselves on most matters, the 'socialist' colonels and 'progressive' sheiks who ruled the Arab world could always find themselves in agreement on one point: their desire to annihilate Israel . . . to wipe Israel off the map . . . to cast the Jews into the sea . . . to put an end to Zionist existence by force. And to attain this objective, they concentrated on preparation for war – largely at the expense of their own national interests. Propaganda campaigns were an essential feature of these preparations, and the 'hate Israel' campaign initiated after 1956 steadily grew in intensity and virulence. Pamphlets, films, television, radio and even school texts were used to foment the 'ideological' campaign against Israel.

But Arab hostility was not confined to the campaign of words. It was accompanied by an irregular war of familiar style. From the Syrian heights above Galilee the occasional mortar bomb or an artillery shell fell on an Israeli settlement; saboteurs laid mines on roads inside Israel, cut telephone lines, or severed water pipes; whilst terrorist 'commandos' staged night ambushes – killing a solitary farmer here, another there. There were few casualties but the situation was unsettling; moreover it was getting worse. Terrorists of the sinister Fatah (the Arabic word for 'conquest' is formed by the letters FTH, hence *Fatah*, letters which reversed form the Arabic word 'death') organisation operating from Syria were trying to get a foothold in the Arab villages within Israel to establish guerilla bases there. All this was at a time when Israel was suffering an economic depression, and immigration was falling off. US aid had been cut back, Zionist fund raising organisations were finding it increasingly more difficult to obtain money overseas, German reparations had ended, and ten per cent of Israeli

Israel's Prime Minister Levi Eshkol talks with some of his generals

Foreign Minister Abba Eban

workers were unemployed.

By the beginning of 1967 all northern Israel smarted from the pinpricks of the guerillas and public opinion was demanding military reprisals, against Syria in particular. But Israel's Prime Minister, Levi Eshkol, and his new Foreign Minister, Abba Eban, preferred diplomacy to militant action. Eshkol had plenty of domestic troubles, especially with inflation and unemployment, and he did not want to add to them by provoking war with the Arabs. Nor did he wish to offend the Soviet Union, which was in an anti-Israel mood. Another important reason for treading carefully was Egypt's military strength, which had recently been augmented by large quantities of modern Soviet Weapons. So the terrorist raids directed by Syria continued until they reached a stage in April when Eshkol was persuaded to authorize a raid. From then on tempers rose, the tension between Israel and the Arab world steadily increased and President Gamal Abdul Nasser began the brinkmanship in the fatal game which got out of control.

'It was not we who started the crisis', protested Nasser after the war. 'We all know that this crisis began with Israel's attempt to invade Syria . . . in that attempt Israel was not working for itself alone but also for the forces that had got impatient with the Arab revolutionary movement . . .' This was probably what the leader of the United Arab Republic, formed originally 'with the object of liberating the Arab homeland from the Zionist peril', genuinely believed at the beginning of the crisis – that Israel was planning a military strike against Syria which would topple the Baathist government in Damascus and so, perhaps, bring an end to Fatah's operations. Nasser felt that he could not afford to stand by and let this happen; hence the claim that his first moves were merely an attempt to deter the Israelis from attacking Syria.

7th April 1967 may be set as the

The Egyptian President Abdul Nasser

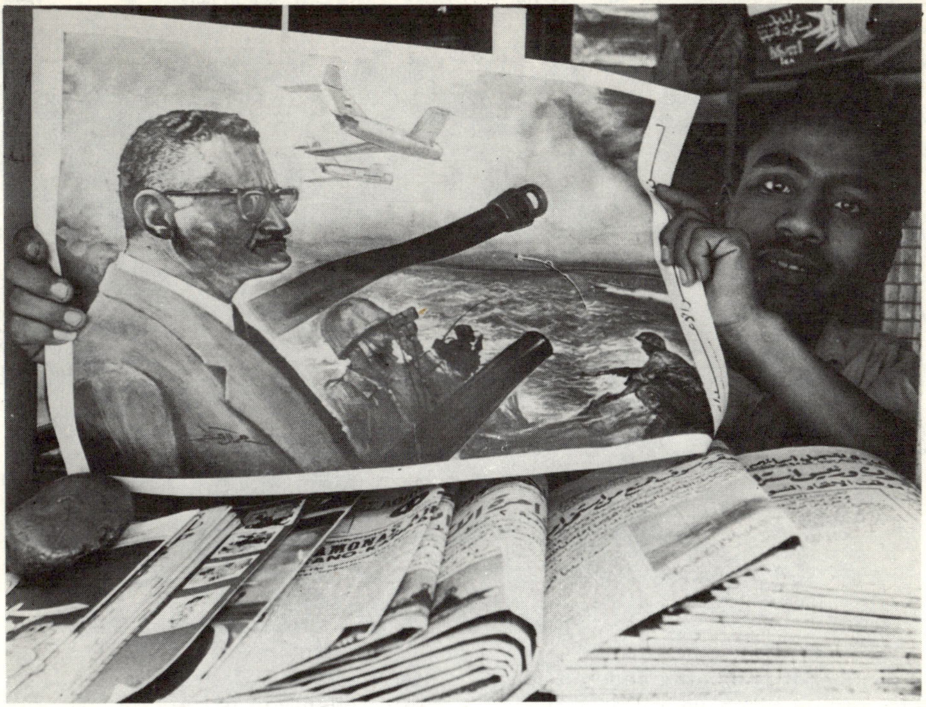

The popular view of President Nasser, seen as a man of strength in a Cairo newsboy's poster

starting point of the crisis. On that day the Syrian guns opened fire on Israeli farmers working in the border settlements of Haon, Ein Gev and Gadot. The settlements were in a disputed border region, but the Syrians had not previously interfered with their cultivation. Israeli machine guns returned the fire and a battle involving tanks, heavy mortars and artillery rapidly developed. Aircraft of the Israeli Air Force were called into action to silence the Syrian guns, and Syrian jet fighters also appeared. An aerial dogfight ensued, in the course of which six Syrian MIGs were shot down. Some of the Israeli Mirages then flew on the fifty or so miles to Damascus to demonstrate their superiority in Syria's air space. Largely because of this loss of face Nasser sent the commander-in-chief of the UAR Air Force to Damascus to discuss Egyptian cooperation with Syria in any future incident. As a result of this visit mutual pledges of joint action against Israeli aggression were announced.

The next step up in the crisis came in the middle of May. During the first week of the month the Fatah made two attacks inside Israel which showed a higher degree of professional training and equipment than hitherto. This was noted with concern not only by the Israelis but also by the UN Secretary-General U Thant. During the next few days two developments then combined to precipitate the second phase of the crisis. The first emanated either directly from Moscow or was concocted in the Soviet Embassy in Tel Aviv. According to the Russians the Israeli troops were concentrating on the Syrian border, and this information was duly passed to Cairo. The second development arose from statements made by Prime Minister Levi Eshkol, and General Yizhak Rabin, the Israeli

A member of a Kibbutz stands outside his quarters which were attacked by Syrian mortar fire, April 1967

Army's chief of staff, on 12th and 13th May. Construed by Nasser as confirmation of the Russian reports, the UAR leader decided that an Israeli attack on Syria was imminent.

In the event not only was there absolutely no truth in the Soviet stories, there was also some doubt that either Eshkol or Rabin said what Nasser was told they had said. Both the Israelis and the UN observers on the Syrian frontier denied the existence of any build up of Israeli troops, and Eshkol even invited the Soviet Ambassador to tour Israel's norther border with him and see the truth for himself. In the event the Ambassador declined. But the damage had been done and, despite a statement by U Thant on 19th May to the effect that there was no sign of any of the alleged concentrations of Israeli troops on the Syrian border, Nasser appears to have been convinced that 'eleven to thirteen' Israeli brigades were there. In a message to a Palestine Day rally of Arab students in Britain on 14th May his theme was that the 'Arab revolution' was faced with a coordinated conspiracy in which US and British 'imperialism' was acting together with both Israel and 'Arab reaction'. ('Arab reaction' referred to King Hussein of Jordan, who was at loggerheads with Syria over the activities of the Fatah terrorists, and who refused to allow Egyptian troops to be stationed in his country.)

Against this melodramatic and almost paranoid picture of a powerful imperialist threat to the Arab world, Nasser's reaction to the reports of Israeli troop concentrations was prompt and fateful. Lieutenant-General Mohammed Fawzi, the Egyptian Army's Chief of Staff, who had been nominated to command the joint Egyptian and Syrian forces in the event of hostilities with Israel, was sent post-haste to Damascus to confer with Syrian Ministers and senior Syrian officers. And amid great publicity, on 15th May, large formations of the Egyptian army began to

Lieutenant-General Mohammed Fawzi, Chief of Staff of the Egyptian army

cross the Suez Canal to take up positions in the Sinai desert. Before 15th May there were less than two UAR infantry divisions and only a small amount of armour in Sinai; within a week there were four divisions. Then, on 16th May, a message from Nasser was delivered to Major-General Rikhye the Indian commander of the UN Emergency Force in Sinai and the Gaza strip. 'I have instructed the armed forces of the United Arab Republic to be prepared for action against Israel the moment the latter carries out an act of aggression against any Arab state. In the light of these orders our forces have been concentrated in Sinai on our eastern frontier. To ensure the complete safety of all UN forces in observation points along our borders, we request that these forces be removed at once.' UN personnel in Gaza and Sinai should be concentrated in the interior of the Gaza strip; nothing was said at this stage about the UN posts at Sabha and on Sharm el-Sheikh, whose guns could command the strait that is Israel's only back door and access to Africa and Asia.

Rikhye objected to the demand on the grounds that it was irregular. But he sent it on to the UN headquarters. While it was being considered in New York on 17th May, Egyptian soldiers were trying to jostle the UNEF troops out of their positions and by that evening they had been turned out of their observation post at Sabha. Next day they were evicted from positions near Kuntilla and several other points in Sinai, and the UNEF commander at Sharm el-Sheikh was brusquely ordered to withdraw his men. Simulteneously with these moves Mahmoud Riad, the Egyptian Foreign Minister, cabled U Thant formally demanding the urgent removal of the UNEF. Anticipating this demand, the UN Secretary-General had already consulted representatives of the countries providing the UNEF contingents, and Canada, India and Yugoslavia had intimated that they would evacuate

General Yizhak Rabin, Chief of Staff in the Israeli army

their men as soon as they were officially asked to do so. Israel had also been asked if she would allow the UNEF to operate on the Israeli side of the frontier, but she had declined. Thus, after voicing 'serious misgivings', U Thant ordered General Rikhye to remove the UN troops and concentrate them in Gaza. Most of them had been withdrawn by the evening of 18th May; only the detachment at Sharm el-Sheikh remained in position and it too packed up and left on the 23rd.

This sudden and dramatic departure of the UNEF came as a shock to the world in general, and to Israel in particular. Since the Suez debacle in 1956 the presence of the UNEF had succeeded in preventing hostilities between Egypt and Israel. It had also assured the free passage of Israeli and other ships through the Straits of Tiran and the Gulf of Akaba into Eilat, the southern port vital to Israel's economy. 90 per cent of Israel's oil supply came from Iran in tankers which discharged their cargoes at Eilat so the importance of free passage through the Akaba Gulf could not be overestimated. Whether Nasser was legally within his rights in demanding the withdrawal of the UNEF, and whether U Thant was wise to agree with so little argument, are questions which are still debated. Nasser himself, who expected to have to bargain and bully over his demand, was taken by surprise when U Thant agreed so readily. In retrospect it seems that legality was on Nasser's side, and from a practical point of view it is quite certain that the UNEF could not have operated with-

out the consent of the Egyptians. Nevertheless, when the UNEF was withdrawn from Sharm el-Sheikh, and Eilat was threatened with strangulation, war between Israel and the UAR became a certainty.

For a few days nothing seemed to happen; to the rest of the world the Middle East was still simmering but it had not yet boiled, and with the moderate and compromising Levi Eshkol in charge of Israel's affairs there seemed to be a good chance of the crisis blowing over. But tension was mounting on both sides. On Monday 22nd May, Eshkol told the Knesset that he had authorized a partial call-up of Israeli reservists to meet the 'grave developments' on Israel's southern border. With many men absent from their daily jobs the Israeli public was already aware that their army was mobilizing. In Cairo, as Egyptian reinforcements continued to pour into Sinai, the Egyptian Government announced that the UAR was also mobilizing, and Ahmed Shukairy told a press conference that his '8,000-strong' Palestine Liberation Army – banned in Jordan – had been placed under the national commands of Egypt, Syria and Iraq. Anxious not to be left out of the drama, Jordan also volunteered to place its armed forces under joint UAR-Syrian command, but Nasser pointedly ignored the offer.

Meantime U Thant had set out from New York to try to persuade Nasser to cool the situation. While he was still on his way to Cairo, the UAR leaders took the fatal step which escalated the crisis into its next phase and made war inevitable. The Straits of Tiran would be closed to ships flying the Israeli flag, Nasser announced. '. . . Under no circumstances will we allow the Israeli flag to pass through the Akaba Gulf. The Jews threatened war. We tell them, we are ready for war. Our armed forces and all our people are ready for war but under no circumstances will we abandon any of our rights. This water is ours . . .' Legally, this was not true. In 1957 the United States and other Western Powers had supported Israel's contention that the Straits of Tiran were an international waterway, and this view was reinforced by the 1958 High Seas Convention. Egypt, however, had never accepted this, and had not been a party to the High Seas Convention. In any case Nasser was not particularly concerned about the international view about the legality of rights of passage. Closing the Straits was a move calculated to send his stock rocketing throughout the Arab

Major-General Rikhye, Indian commander of the United Nations Emergency Force, withdraws his officers from the King's Gate border post

Above: Israel's reserve army assembles. *Below:* Israel's women soldiers prepare to play their part in the coming conflict. *Right:* Ahmed Shukairy, chief of the Palestine Liberation Army

world and Egyptians, demonstrating in Cairo and Alexandria, roared their approval. Those who appreciated that their President was playing with fire trusted his judgement, and hoped that he had got away with a political coup without the need for any fighting. Tunisia and Saudi Arabia, the least militant of the so-called Arab world, expressed their support and acclaim; Algeria proclaimed a state of alert and former FLN fighters were asked to volunteer for service in the struggle against 'Zionism'. Only Jordan, whose quarrel with Syria had intensified when a terrorist's bomb exploded in a bus at a Jordanian border post, abstained from the rush to demonstrate Arab unity and approval of Nasser's action.

The Israelis' reaction to Nasser's announcement was one of alarm and despondency. One Israeli doctor was approached by a middle-aged woman who wanted suicide pills to take if necessary – she had lived through one of Hitler's concentration camps and felt she could not live through anything similar. A father told of his ten-year-old son returning home from school saying that if the Israeli Government would not fight he did not wish to be an Israeli any more – he would go to America and become an American. The Israeli press clamoured for action and Eshkol took the

unusual step of consulting the leaders of the opposition parties. Lack of confidence in his government was growing and anxiety was rising even in the Israeli forces. People were calling for changes in the government – for a new Defence Minister and a new Prime Minister in particular. Meanwhile provocative propaganda broadcast from Cairo and other Arab radio stations was preparing public opinion for war and promising death and extermination to Israel. 'All Egypt is now prepared to plunge into total war which will put an end to Israel' declared the *Saut-al Arab* commentator on 17th May. 'Our basic objective will be the destruction of Israel. The Arab people want to fight' said President Nasser on 27th May. And Ahmed Shukairy is reported to have said that any Jews who managed to survive the war which was imminent would be allowed to stay in Palestine – but he did not expect many to survive.

Against this background the Israeli military leaders, headed by General Rabin, began to urge their government to authorize immediate military action. But the Knesset was divided about the risks of resorting to arms immediately. Influenced by a message from President Lyndon Johnson advising restraint, and asking the Israelis to refrain from any attempt to force the Egyptian blockade of the Straits of Tiran for forty-eight hours, the Israeli Government decided to try diplomacy first. So it was decided that their Foreign Minister, Abba Eban, should go to Washington to see President Johnson, travelling by way of Paris and London. Meantime, in Washington, the American president had issued a vague statement to the effect that the US regarded the closing of the Gulf of Akaba and a blockade of Israeli shipping as 'illegal and potentially dangerous to peace'. The Soviet Union, who took longer to appreciate the inherent dangers in the worsening situation, issued a statement attributing the crisis to Israeli designs on Syria. But the Russians made no reference to the Gulf of Akaba and according to French sources, the Egyptian and Syrian ambassadors in Moscow were told that the Soviet Union was not prepared to risk a confrontation with the United States by giving military support to the UAR if a war with Israel came about. On 26th May, when reports reached Moscow to the effect that both Egypt and Israel believed an attack on the other was imminent, the Soviet Union sent an urgent warning to both Nasser and Eshkol

PLA troops during training in Syria

against taking military action.

In the three days which had elapsed since Nasser announced his blockade of the Akaba Gulf the situation had certainly deteriorated. On 24th May an Egyptian spokesman declared that Nasser's announcement had been implemented: the Straits of Tiran had been closed the previous day by mines and guns, and that the Egyptian Navy and aircraft of the Egyptian Air Force were patrolling the area. Israeli ships approaching the Straits would be fired on; all others would be stopped and searched. Another announcement reported the arrival in Egypt of an advance party of Kuwaiti troops, some Sudanese military personnel and an Algerian military mission. U Thant, now in Cairo, was told by Nasser that the UAR would not strike the first blow, but if Israel wanted peace she would have to give up certain territory, including Eilat, and recognize that the Gulf of Akaba was Egyptian waters. Meanwhile, Jordan, believing that her future depended on her cooperation with the rest of the Arab world in the crisis, was still intent on getting into the picture, and Jordanian troops, tanks and guns were moved to the Israeli frontier with the same flurry of publicity as was given to the moves of Egyptian formations. A Government spokesman in Amman also announced

that Saudi Arabian troops had arrived in Jordan, that more were expected, and that permission had also been given for Iraqi troops to enter the country. In the event no Saudi Arabian troops had arrived, and the Iraqis had no intention of sending troops to support Jordan while King Hussein remained in power. Nor did Nasser seem keen to admit Jordan to the UAR fold, since fresh gestures by Jordan promising cooperation with Egypt were ignored.

From the Israelis' viewpoint the situation was terrifying. If 80 million Arabs really had united for war, and if they struck simultaneously on all fronts before Israel was fully mobilized, they might well achieve the objective which Nasser had said on 27th May was '. . . the destruction of Israel'. Clearly, neither the US, Britain nor France had any real intention of honouring the pledges they had made to keep the Straits of Tiran open, and if and when it came to the crunch it seemed unlikely that they would give any other help. The United States was canvassing support for an international naval force, irreverently known as 'The Red Sea Regatta', to escort ships through the Straits of Tiran and the Akaba Gulf, but there was little real enthusiasm for the idea. The truth was that none of the Great Powers wanted to get involved: Israel was on her own. France, the United States and the Soviet Union all warned both Israel and Egypt against shooting first, and it was the increasing fears of either side that the other might strike the first blow which escalated the crisis to its final stage. The Chiefs of Staff of the Israeli Forces were now pressing for quick action, arguing that every day's delay would mean more Israeli casualties in a war which had become inevitable. When the Israeli Cabinet met on 28th May after hearing Abba Eban's report on his visit to Paris, London and Washington, they deferred a decision on going to war. But Israeli criticism of the Government's inactivity was growing and public opinion was clamouring for a more militant policy and for a more vigorous leadership. This eventually crystallised round General Moshe Dayan, the dashing Cyclops, who had earned the sobriquet 'Hero of Sinai' in 1956. Despite Eshkol's opposition, Dayan was appointed Minister of Defence with General Zvi Zur as his deputy.

Perhaps the most spectacular development at this time was King Hussein's sudden decision to fly to Cairo and sign a joint defence agreement with his old enemy, Nasser. The

U Thant visits Cairo in an effort to avert the crisis

Israel's well-equipped armoured units take up their positions in the deserts shortly before the outbreak of hostilities

Members of Jordan's Arab Legion stand guard in the old City of Jerusalem

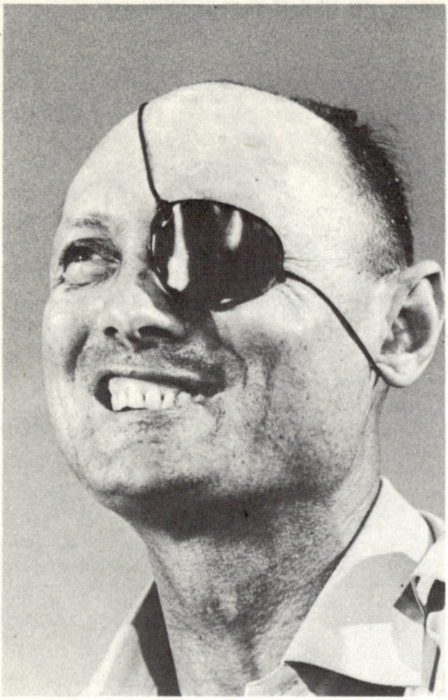

Above: General Moshe Dayan, Israel's new Minister of Defence. _Below:_ King Hussein and President Nasser sign their joint defence agreement

journey was made in great secrecy. 'What would happen if we arrested you' Nasser asked him on his arrival in Cairo. 'Such an eventuality never disturbed me', the King replied. Under the terms of the agreement Jordan's armed forces were placed under the command of an Egyptian general, Major-General Abdul Munim Riad, and Iraqi and other Arab troops were permitted to enter Jordan. The immediate outcome was that two battalions of Egyptian paratroops were flown to Jordan and Hussein announced that Jordan had joined Egypt in 'the holy war'. From Iraq it was also announced that an Iraqi division was marching to Jordan to support Jordan's Arab Legion. More surprising, and perhaps more alarming to the Israelis, was that Ahmed Shukairy accompanied Hussein back to Jordan.

The new military link-up between Egypt, Jordan and Syria could not have made any significant difference to the military balance for some time to come. But the threat of encircle-

Popular feeling begins to boil up in Egypt as Palestine Liberation Army volunteers turn out for war service

ment, however ineffective in the short run, was enough to convince the majority of Israelis that the Arabs were preparing to attack. It also undermined the arguments of those among the Israeli political leaders who were still advocating waiting while continuing diplomatic efforts to deal with the blockade of the Straits of Tiran. On both sides, diplomacy was now fighting a losing battle with public passions and military fears, and the original cause of the dispute, the closure of the Straits, became overshadowed by military considerations. Arabs and Israelis alike both felt that they might lose the advantage by delay, or that the other side might gain advantage by striking first. This was especially so among the Israelis, since Israel's strategy was based on a swift offensive. Most Israelis wanted to get the ordeal over with rather than wait for an Arab attack or for their country's economy to be slowly strangled. In Cairo the mood was somewhat more fatalistic. The Egyptians were crossing their fingers as much as anyone else, and hoping that Nasser had got away with a political coup without the need for war. But they knew that Israel might attack at any time and many were uneasy about the outcome if it did come to war.

Nasser himself was undecided about the next move. He had promised both Moscow and Washington that he would not fire the first shot, and he did not know how the US 6th Fleet would react if he did. Nor did he know how much support, if any, he would get from the Soviet Union if he struck first. Neither did he appreciate the readiness and ability of the Israelis, especially the Dayan generation, to go it alone. This, and his over-optimistic picture of Egyptian military power, were the most serious miscalculations he made.

While Nasser dithered, the Israelis

were making rapid preparations for war. On Saturday 3rd June, Moshe Dayan gave the first press conference since the announcement of his appointment as Defence Minister, and made a conciliatory and disarming statement. The Government was trying to bring about a diplomatic settlement, he said, and their efforts must be given a chance. Asked if Israel had lost the military initiative, he replied: 'If you mean to say we stand no chance then I cannot agree with you.' Elsewhere publicity was deliberately being given to Israeli troops on weekend leave, sporting on the beaches. Finally, that evening, the Israeli Cabinet met to decide whether to continue to wait in the hope that diplomacy and good sense might still yield a peaceful solution – delay which might mean annihilation; or let the army decide time, place, and method of response to an Arab attack. Seventeen men met that afternoon and fifteen voted in favour of an immediate war against Egypt.

Men of the Palestine Liberation Army with their 'Death to Israel' banner

Israel's secret preparations were in vivid contrast with the blare of publicity which attended those of the Arabs. In Cairo the Libyan Foreign Minister declared on 4th June that Libyan troops would be coming to fight alongside the Egyptians, and that the Americans would not be permitted to use the Wheelers Air Base if they tried to help the 'Zionists'. Meantime General Riad had assumed command of Hussein's army, and a brigade of the division which Iraq had said was marching to Jordan arrived on the northern border of that country. A Saudi Arabian brigade had also crossed into Jordan and two others, encamped near Akaba, were expected to move into Hussein's territory the following day. Some of the Western Powers were still trying to find a solution, but the diplomatic battle had been lost; this was the eve of war.

Strategy and relative strengths

A parallel has often been drawn between the war in Israel and the conflict of David against Goliath: two million Jews against eighty million Arabs. In 1967 Goliath was equipped with the most modern weapons but was still living in the Middle Ages, whereas David – for all his fragile appearance and sometimes out of date armament – had already reached the electronic age. In the two decades which had elapsed since the State of Israel was born, the Israeli Defence Forces (IDF) had come a long way. The army, evolved mainly from Haganah of Mandate times, had been expanded and organised on conventional lines; conscription meant that practically every Israeli citizen, including women, would serve in its ranks. From a motley collection of obsolescent planes of the Second World War the Israeli Air Force was built up into a formidable fighting machine. Without the cooperation and friendship of France during the 1950s this might not have been pos-

Fouga Magister planes of Israel's air force

sible. Prompted by the attitude of Egypt towards the Algerian rebels, the French supplied Israel with aircraft and arms, and by 1967 well over half of the planes of the Israeli Air Force were French – and most of the remainder were French designed Fouga Magisters which had been assembled in a factory set up in Israel by the French firm of Fouga. Because it was allocated almost half the Israeli defence budget of over $350 million and its dedicated professional pilots were the cream of Israeli manpower, the air force was the elite component of the IDF. The navy, on the other hand, was the poor relation. Based on Haifa, Ashdod and Eilat, it had only about twenty-four ships and its total manpower was no more than 3,000. Of the three services it was the army which the Israelis regarded as the main bulwark against Arab aggression, and in the event of war the role of the air force – and to a lesser extent the navy – was to support the army's operations. Control,

Young people of a Kibbutz fill sand bags to build a guard post near the Jordanian frontier

direction and coordination of military policy and operations was the responsibility of the Israeli General Staff, the Chief of Staff being directly responsible for all three Services to the Minister of Defence. In principle the military was subordinate to the civilian authority of the Israeli Government. From the earliest days of the founding of the State, however, the IDF had enjoyed a special relationship with its civilian masters. This permitted the Chief of Staff a freedom of action not enjoyed by his contemporaries in any Western democracy. Living in an atmosphere of uncertainty and terrorism, surrounded by hostile peoples who were continually promising 'the final liquidation of Zionist existence', the need to be able to act rapidly and decisively can be seen as ample justification for this special privilege accorded to the military.

Israel, being a small country with no depth, was unsuitable for fighting defensive battles, and the strategy evolved by the General Staff depended wholly on offensive action outside its borders. In 1967 the main threat was seen to be Egypt whose armed forces had been reinforced and strengthened to an unprecedented degree by huge shipments of arms from the Soviet Union. The regimes in neighbouring Jordan and Syria were scarcely stable, and Lebanon had no military strength worth reckoning with. King Hussein's Arab Legion had fought well on previous occasions but it was unlikely that Hussein would order them to attack Israel, and it seemed equally unlikely that the Syrians would leave the security of their strongly entrenched positions on the Golan plateau. Thus, if war came, the Israeli policy was to parry any move by Jordan and Syria – and Lebanon if need be – while concentrating on the defeat of Egypt. Then, when Egypt had been dealt with the IDF troops could turn on Jordan and Syria; the object being not to fight on more than one front at a time. If this strategy brought success, an outcry from the Arab world and those who sympathised with it would undoubtedly result in pressure for a cease-fire by the United Nations collectively, or some of its powerful members individually. The Israelis could therefore reckon on no more than a few days to attain their objectives, and the IDF General Staff plans were based on a three-day campaign. After that economic sanctions and shortages of food, fuel and the material with which to continue would compel the operations to be halted. On this premise the training of Israeli troops focussed on a three-day period of continuous campaigning, fighting night and day; and Israeli brigades were organised as self-contained formations equipped with three days' fuel

Students in Tel Aviv help prepare for war by digging trenches

and supplies.

From a population of over two million Israel was able to mobilize a total force of 264,000 within seventy-two hours. The mobilization procedure was flexible, and its extent depended on the degree of an emergency. Economic difficulties resulting from the closure of factories or the shortage of labour on the kibbutzim would clearly follow if complete mobilization was to last more than a few days. So once the Israeli Government had decided that war was inevitable, any doubts about its inevitability had to be discarded. When conscription was ordered, war must follow, because Israel could not afford to stand-to indefinitely, while demobilization would probably be interpreted by the Arabs as a sign of weakness.

Each reservist kept his uniform at home, and mobilization orders summoning him to report at a collection centre were issued in the form of a code message over the radio. Special arrangements were made to collect key men such as unit commanders and staff officers; the remainder reported to a nearby collection centre from where they were taken to the base camp at which their unit was assembling and where arms and equipment were issued. The mobilization routine had been practised so many times that it was almost perfect. When the Six-Day War began three-quarters of Israel's reserves had been mobilized, and on the morning of the first day the code names of the remaining units were read out over the radio: Love of Zion, Close Shave, Men of Work, Alternating Current, Open Window, Good Fields. Throughout Israel the youths and middle-aged men comprising these units scrambled into the streets with their bundles and knapsacks, heading for their prearranged rendezvous with the buses which would take them to the base

An infantry unit moves up to the front line near Jerusalem

Troops in the desert near the Jordan frontier take their midday meal

camps.

In normal times Israel's standing army comprised 2,000 regulars and up to 72,000 conscripts and reservists undergoing training. Some of these men were at basic training centres, but the majority were organised into seven brigades, each roughly equivalent in size and organisation to an American regiment. Of these seven four were 'conventional' infantry, one other infantry brigade was trained in the paratroop role, and the other two were armoured formations. When the army was fully mobilized there were 31 brigades – 22 of which were infantry, eight armoured, and the one élite paratroop formation. Each infantry brigade had about 4,500 men, and the armoured brigades were about 3,500 strong; two of the reserve infantry brigades had also been trained as paratroopers. The percentage rates of 'teeth' to 'tail' was thus in the order of 50:50, which compares very favourably with the ratio of 20:80 (or more) in the armies of the United States and Britain.

The brigades were the basic formations in the Israeli army, and they were not constituted into divisions. For a special operation, however, several brigades could be grouped into a task force known as an *Ugda*. A number of *Ugdas* were formed during the Six Day War, and command of these was given to officers whose peaceful appointments had lapsed with the onset of hostilities. These included Brigadier Eiad Peled, Commandant of the National Defence College, Brigadier Ariel Sharon, Director of Military Training, and such officers as Brigadier Uzi Narkiss, commander of Israel's Northern Com-

Brigadier Ariel Sharon

\ column of half-tracks carries Israeli roops to the front line

nand, Brigadier Yeshayshu Garvish, :ommander of Southern Command, ınd Brigadier Israel Tal, the Arnoured Corps commander; Brigadier ∖vraham Yoffe – 'Gideon' in the War)f Independence – was called out of 'eserve to command an *Ugda* in Sinai, vhere he had distinguished himself n 1956.

With the accent on offensive action ınd mobility, the infantry battalions · three of which were organic to each nfantry brigade – were all motorized. The armoured brigades, usually com-)rising two tank battalions and one nfantry battalion carried in arnoured half-tracks, were equipped vith a variety of tanks of British, American and French origin. In round figures the total number of tanks available was about 250 Centurions, 200 M-48 Pattons, 150 AMX-13s and 200 'Super'-Shermans, all of which had been adapted for war in the desert. The Super-Sherman was basically the old American 30-ton M-4 Sherman of the Second World War, modified and rebuilt, with a more powerful engine, a 76mm gun and broader tracks. The 14.5-ton French AMX-13, a fast and manoeuvrable light tank, had a 75mm or 40mm gun and carried French SS10 or SS11 guided anti-tank missiles. The powerful 45-ton Pattons, with maximum speed of 35mph and high-velocity

Israeli crews mount their Centurion tanks during training

Above and below: **Modernised and modified Shermans of the Israeli armoured corps**

90mm guns, were the same tanks as those which until comparatively recently had been the main battle tank of the US army. As such they were one of the most powerful tanks in the Middle East; only the 50-ton British Centurions were superior in armament and armour, and they were much slower. These were Mark V and Mark VI models, fitted with 105mm guns in place of their original 20 pounders.

In addition to the 800 tanks of the types described Israel also had about 250 self-propelled guns – 155mm howitzers mounted on Sherman chassis, and 105mm howitzers mounted on AMX-13s. Infantry weapons were of conventional types – many of them being of Second World War vintage. But there were plenty of 120mm and smaller calibre mortars, and locally manufactured Uzi sub-machine guns.

The Israeli Air Force, when finally mobilized, amounted to about 20,000. Before the war started Israel possessed about 450 aircraft of which

A 120mm mortar mounted on an Israeli half-track

350 could be classed as first-line and operational machines. These were divided into thirteen squadrons – four of interceptors, five of fighter-bombers, two of transport aircraft, and two of helicopters. Having no long-range bombers, there was no strategic bomber force, and as the range of most of the Israeli planes was limited to about 400 miles or less, large areas of Egypt, Iraq and Saudi Arabia were beyond their reach. Of the 350 operational planes there were 20 French Super Mystère fighter-bombers, between 40 and 60 of the earlier Mystère Mark IVA ground attack fighters which were about ten years old, 73 Mirage Mark III supersonic interceptor/ground-attack fighters, 48 obsolescent Duragan fighter-bombers, 60 of the locally assembled Fouga Magisters, modified for use as ground-attack fighter-bombers, 25 Vatour ground-attack bombers, 20 Noratlas and

Stratocruiser transports – each capable of carrying some 45 combat soldiers or 18 stretcher cases, and approximately 25 assorted helicopters. Of these planes only the Mirage interceptors and the Super-Mystères were considered capable of challenging the Egyptian MiG-21s supplied by the Soviet Union. Technically all these types of planes were an approximate match. All were supersonic; all were fitted with 30mm cannon and carried air-to-air missiles. Schooled by their Russian instructors, however, the Egyptian pilots firmly believed that their MiG-21s were superior to anything the Israelis could put into the air; time was to show that the training and skills of the Israeli pilots would compensate for any technical differences between the Soviet and French designed aircraft.

On 'the other side of the hill', the four Arab nations under Egyptian military command had recently been equipped with large quantities of some of the most modern weapons in the world. Egypt itself had an army which in terms of armoured might and destructive capacity rivalled that of the German Wehrmacht which crushed France in May 1940. Supporting this army was a large up-to-date air force, and a navy possessing the most powerful fleet of any Mediterranean country except France. Jordan, Syria and Iraq were less powerful adversaries; oil-rich Kuwait which sent a brigade to the canal zone when the war started,

Mirage IIIs of the Israeli air force

Algeria which sent another brigade and three squadrons of MiGs, Saudi Arabia which also contributed a brigade and the Sudan which pledged troops but never sent them, could be judged even less of a menace on their own. But the combined order of battle of Egypt, Jordan, Syria and Iraq consisted of over 400,000 men, 2,700 tanks and more than 700 aircraft – backed up by a comprehensive logistic organisation, and training in Soviet military methods.

Following the Egyptian army's shattering defeat by the Israelis in the Sinai campaign of 1956 the Soviet Union started to re-arm the Arabs. Between 1957 and 1967 some $1,000 million of arms and equipment was sent to Egypt – many of the latest types of weapons being sent to Egypt before the demands of Soviet Eastern Bloc allies had been satisfied. All this material was supplied to the Arab countries for a fraction of the cost of its Western equivalent, and on generous long term payments in local currency. Along with the equipment came hundreds of Russian instructors to provide technical advice and to teach Soviet strategy and tactics. By 1960 the Egyptian army had become, on paper anyway, the most powerful in the Middle East, and it was still growing. By 1967 Egypt possessed about 1,200 tanks, 200 self-propelled guns, 1,200 armoured personnel carriers and over 1,000 conventional guns. Most of the armour was Russian – nearly a thousand of the tanks being versions of the famous 32-ton T-34 of the Second World War. The original T-34, of which the Egyptians had received about 450, was equipped with an 85mm gun capable of a high rate of fire but lacking adequate means of fire-control. The T-54, of which there were about 300, was an upgunned version of the T-34; and the T-55, of which the Egyptians possessed some 200, was an improved and modified T-54. Like its predecessor, which was the standard tank of the Soviet army, the T-55 carried a gyro-stabilized 100mm gun, but it had thicker armour and was provided with sophisticated direction-finding and fire-control devices.

Of the remaining tanks the 46-ton Joseph Stalin, JS-3, with its heavy armour and powerful 122mm gun, was the most formidable. 90 American Shermans, 30 British Centurions, 20 French AMX-13s and about 30 others of various age, origin and rôle completed the Egyptian tank armoury. To support this armour the Russians had thoughtfully provided a range of self-propelled guns, including SU-100 'tank destroyers', JSU-152s – which as the name implies mounted a 152mm gun, ASU-57 light anti-tank guns

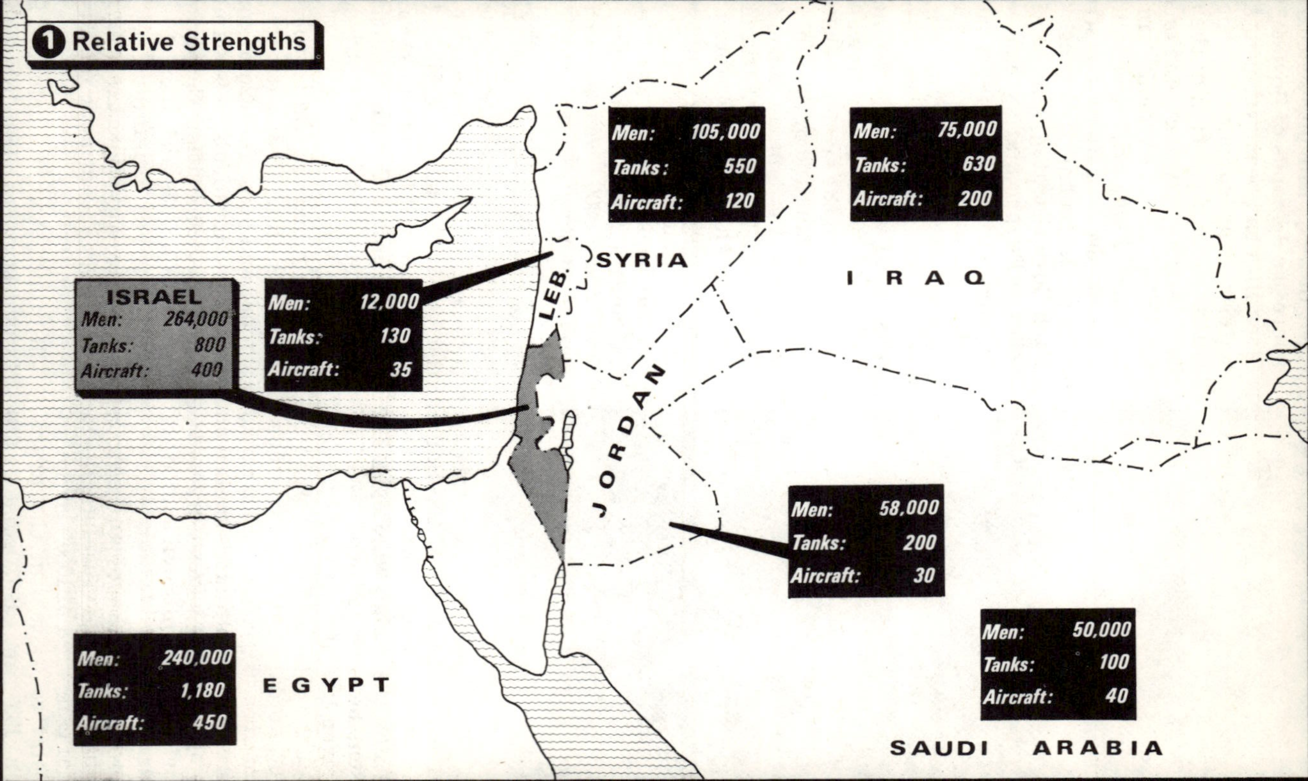

1 Relative Strengths
ISRAEL
Men: 264,000
Tanks: 800
Aircraft: 400
Men: 12,000
Tanks: 130
Aircraft: 35
Men: 105,000
Tanks: 550
Aircraft: 120
Men: 75,000
Tanks: 630
Aircraft: 200
SYRIA
LEB
I R A Q
JORDAN
Men: 58,000
Tanks: 200
Aircraft: 30
Men: 240,000
Tanks: 1,180
Aircraft: 450
E G Y P T
Men: 50,000
Tanks: 100
Aircraft: 40
SAUDI ARABIA

which were capable of being air-transported, and S-57 anti-aircraft tanks mounting twin radar-controlled 57mm AA guns. A wide range of Soviet artillery field pieces was supplied to give additional artillery support; these included 130mm field guns, 122mm howitzers, and 12mm guns. To thicken up their fire the Egyptians were also issued with a few of the old Katyusha truck-mounted rocket-firing vehicles. 57mm, 85mm and 100mm anti-tank guns, supplemented by anti-tank guided missiles mounted on trucks and known as *Schmel*, were provided to counter the Israeli armour. And for the infantry and the supply columns there was the BTR-152 six-wheeled armoured personnel carrier, the BTR-50(P) tracked armoured personnel carrier, as well as a host of the same types of trucks and vehicles as were in current service with the Soviet Army. Infantry weapons such as the mortars, small arms, anti-tank bazookas and grenades included in the Arab hand-out were also the same as those in use in the Russian army.

With a population of 30 millions, expanding at the rate of three-quarters of a million every year, and a three-year conscription period, manpower was no problem for those intent on expanding Egypt's armed forces. But the calibre of the individuals was a drawback. The hardships imposed by his background have given the Egyptian fellah a certain tough endurance, and with patience and good training hc can be turned into a good soldier. But he lacks education, imagination and initiative and these shortcomings, superimposed on language difficulties, did not make the task of the Russian instructors any easier. A shortage of competent regimental officers was another problem. Soviet arms and equipment in Arab hands might well be superior to that of the Israelis, and available in greater abundance, but the exploitation of these advantages necessitated a proper understanding and familiarization with the weapons. In the time available this was not possible. Lack of Soviet experience in desert warfare, exacerbated perhaps by the instructor's own training in tactics more suited to warfare in Eastern Europe, and an inflexible outlook, did not help either.

The fighting element of the Egyptian Army comprised three armoured divisions and four infantry divisions, all organised on the same basis as divisions in the Soviet Army. Each division had the support of two artillery regiments. Additionally there was an independent paratroop brigade and fifteen commando battalions, with a relatively high level of training performance. Two Egyptian commando battalions were flown to Jordan on the eve of the war and these attempted to organise a campaign of terror in Israel's Ramle-Sha'ar Haggai area on the vital road connecting Jerusalem with Tel Aviv.

The Egyptian Air Force was about the same size as the Israeli Air Force. but its aircraft were more modern and almost all of Soviet origin. By types these consisted of about 130 of the latest MiG-21 fighters, 80 MiG-19s, 180 of the earlier MiG-17s and original MiG-15s, 20 SU-7 fighter-bombers, 30 TU-16 reconnaissance bombers, and 40 Ilyushin-28s. There were also about 90 transport planes – Ilyushin-14s and Antonov-12s, as well as about 60 helicopters. Some of these were in the Yemen, supporting the Egyptian army fighting there. By the end of May 1967, however, most of them had returned to Egypt.

The combination of Tupolev-bombers with a large MiG aerial umbrella represented a formidable offensive weapon for a first-strike knock-out blow. Acting alone it could deliver 300 tons of high explosives in a single raid on Israeli cities; and if the air forces of Jordan, Syria and Iraq struck with it the overall capacity was 500 tons. The threat represented by the transport aircraft was no less awesome. Under Soviet guidance the

Above: Egyptian tanks are prepared for war in the Sinai desert. *Below:* Maintenance training for men of the Jordanian armoured divisions. *Right:* King Hussein inspects a Jordanian Patton tank

Egyptians had made significant advances in air-landing and air-dropping techniques. Using all their Ilyushins, Antonovs, MI-4 and MI-6 helicopters, they were capable of dropping 3,000 men in one flight and landing another 4,000 together with 600 tons of equipment and supplies. Shielded by a comprehensive radar warning system, as some of whose installations were well forward in the Sinai, and their airfields spread over a wide area, the Egyptians were also much less vulnerable to bombing than the Israelis. Israel's cities and industries were concentrated in a tiny restricted zone, while those of Egypt – with the exception of Cairo – were widely dispersed. In any bombing and counter-bombing contest, therefore, the Israelis would undoubtedly suffer most.

By comparison with that of Israel superiority of the Egyptian Navy was overwhelming. Israel possessed only four destroyers (all ex-British and of Second World War vintage including one, the *Haifa*, captured from the Egyptians in October 1956), two old submarines, an ex-German coastguard cutter, three old American landing craft and 12 motor torpedo boats. Egypt, on the other hand, had a fleet of more than 100 vessels, including eight destroyers – six of which were of the Soviet Skoryo Class; 18 fast Soviet missile boats equipped with Soviet surface-to-surface Styx missiles; and 12 submarines of the Soviet V and R Classes. Three-quarters of this fleet was based on Port Said and Alexandria, and as soon as hostilities

Tank transporters move up to the frontier through a Jordan suburb

commenced Nasser warned all international shipping to keep clear of the Israeli coast.

Like Egypt, the forces of the other Arab states had been built up in the decade prior to 1967. The Jordanian Army, smaller than that of Egypt but the most professional and best-trained of all the Arab armies, was well equipped with modern British and American weapons. Its total strength amounted to about 55,000 organised on the British pattern into seven infantry and two armoured brigades. Each of the latter had two armoured regiments equipped with 40 Patton tanks (M-47s and M-48s) or Centurions; and the infantry element of these brigades were carried in US M-113 armoured personnel carriers, of which America had supplied over 250 as part of $5 million of military aid to Jordan.

Over and above the tanks with the regular armoured regiment there were at least 50 in reserve, and the Israelis claim that Jordan deployed 270 tanks and 150 field guns during the course of the Six Day War. (Some of these 'tanks' were probably other types of armoured vehicles – armoured cars and reconnaissance vehicles of British origin, perhaps). Artillery consisted mainly of British 25 pounder field guns and 17 pounder anti-tank guns, but there were also some 155mm 'Long Toms'.

The Jordanian Air Force was small; it was also very short of pilots, and according to King Hussein there were only 16 pilots for his two squadrons of Hawker Hunter ground attack fighters. Six months before the war broke out America had provided Jordan 36 F104 Starfighters, and six of these had actually been delivered. In the event, with no Jordanian pilots to fly them, however, Hussein asked the American instructors who had flown the Starfighters to Amman, to take them out of his country. Thus the Jordanian air war effort was restricted to twenty-two Hunters, three Doves, three old Dakotas and three helicopters.

Syria's army in 1967 consisted of two armoured brigades, two mechanized brigades and five infantry brigades with a total manpower of about 65,000. Like Egypt's army it had been organised on quasi-Soviet lines and lavishly equipped with Soviet weapons. More than 500 Soviet tanks had been delivered to Syria, most of them T-34s and T-54s; and Syrian artillery was especially well provided with a large variety of Soviet field guns, howitzers, anti-tank guns and mortars. There was also a large number of anti-aircraft guns. The Syrian Air Force, with a strength of approximately 9,000 men, possessed about 120 Soviet aircraft. These were organised into two operational fighter squadrons of MiG-21s and MiG-19s, and two squadrons of MiG-17s. Like Jordan, Iraq and to a lesser extent

One of Jordan's 155mm Long Toms

Egypt, Syria was short of trained pilots and although Soviet instructors had made good progress, the Syrian pilots and ground crews were far from attaining a standard of efficiency approaching that of the Israelis.

The Iraqi Army, which contributed a force of divisional strength to Jordan, numbered about 75,000 regular troops organised on the Soviet pattern into four infantry divisions and one armoured division. As in the other Arab armies their equipment was modern Soviet material, and the Iraqi Air Force of some 220 aircraft boasted two MiG-21 fighter squadrons, three MiG-15 or MiG-17 squadrons, and one squadron each of Tu-16 and Il-18 bombers, as well as transport and helicopter squadrons. Again like the other Arab States, the Iraqis had barely enough trained pilots to fly all the planes which they possessed.

From this brief review of the Israeli and Arab military machines it is clear that the Arabs had the advantage over the Israelis in manpower and equipment. Coupled with the strategic position of Israel vis-a-vis the Arab countries this put the latter in a very strong position. Furthermore the Arabs had declared their aim of seeking a 'Final Solution' to the Palestine problem and the combined military might of Egypt, Syria, Jordan and Iraq was arrayed on the borders of Israel and ready to move. Reinforcements were moving up from Algeria, Kuwait and Saudi Arabia and General Mortaji, the commander of the Egyptian troops in Sinai, issued an Order of the Day declaring 'The eyes of the whole world are upon us in the expectation of seeing the results of our Holy War. With the force of our arms and the unity of our brotherhood, we will conquer the plundered soil of Palestine.'

A T34 (right) of Second World War vintage, with a more recent T54, both shown after their capture by Israeli forces

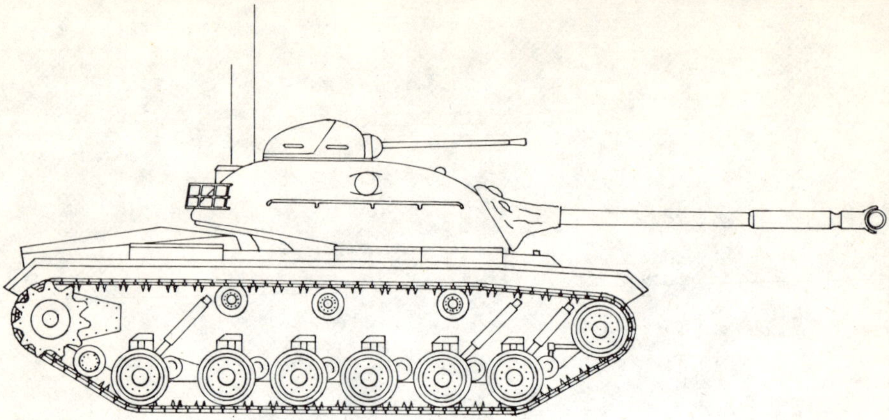

The American M48A2 Patton III medium tank
Weight: **46 tons.** ***Crew:*** **4.** ***Armament:*** **one 90-mm M41 gun with 64 rounds, and one .5-inch and one .3-inch Browning machine guns, with 1,365 and 5,950 rounds respectively.** ***Armour:*** **178-mm maximum, 25-mm minimum.** ***Engine:*** **one Continental AV 1790-7C diesel inline, 810-hp.** ***Speed:*** **30 mph.** ***Range:*** **288 miles.** ***Length:*** **28 feet 6 inches.** ***Width:*** **11 feet 11 inches.** ***Height:*** **10 feet 1⅝ inches.**

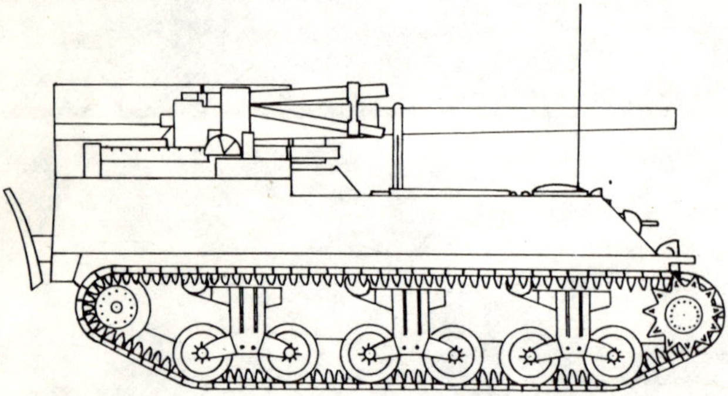

The American/Israeli self-propelled 155-mm howitzer, Sherman chassis
Weight: **27 tons.** ***Crew:*** **5-7.** ***Armament:*** **one 155-mm howitzer and one .3-inch Browning machine gun.** ***Armour:*** **hull front and sides 13-mm.** ***Engine:*** **one Ford GAA inline, 500-hp.** ***Speed:*** **29 mph.** ***Range:*** **150 miles.** ***Length:*** **20 feet 7 inches.** ***Width:*** **8 feet 9 inches.** ***Height:*** **11 feet 11 inches.**

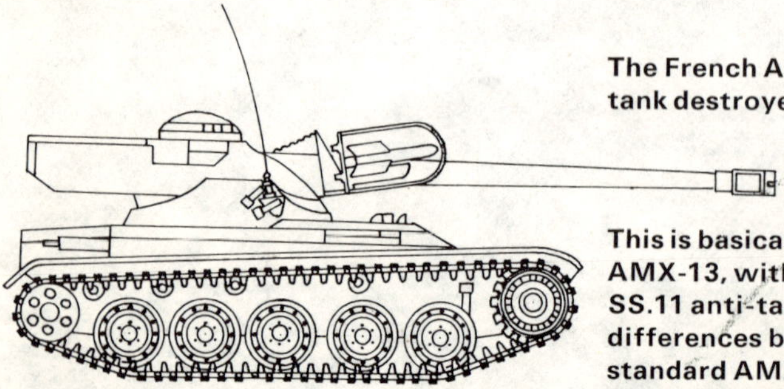

The French AMX-13/SS.11 light tank/ tank destroyer

This is basically the same vehicle as the AMX-13, with four rails for launching SS.11 anti-tank missiles. The only major differences between this vehicle and the standard AMX-13 are increased weight (15.3 tons) and main armament ammunition stowage (33 rounds).

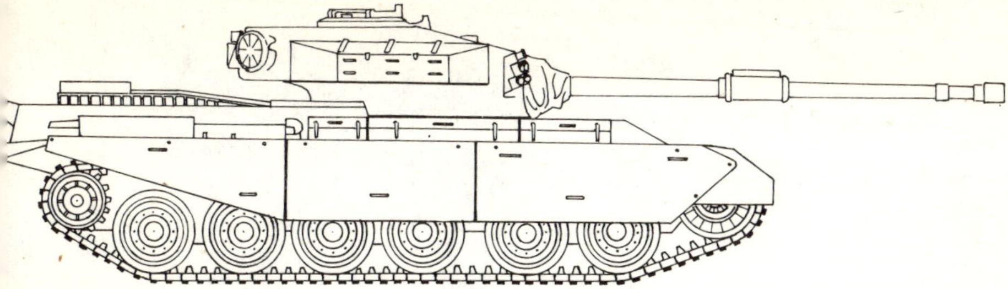

he British Centurion 5/2 medium tank
Veight: 49.5 tons. *Crew:* 4. *Armament:* one 105-mm L7 gun with 64 rounds, and two
3-inch Browning machine guns with 4,250 rounds. *Armour:* 152-mm maximum.
ngine: one Rolls-Royce Meteor IVB inline, 650-hp. *Speed:* 21.5 mph. *Range:*
0 miles (without extra fuel tanks). *Length:* 32 feet 3 inches. *Width:* 11 feet
1½ inches. *Height:* 9 feet 7¾ inches.

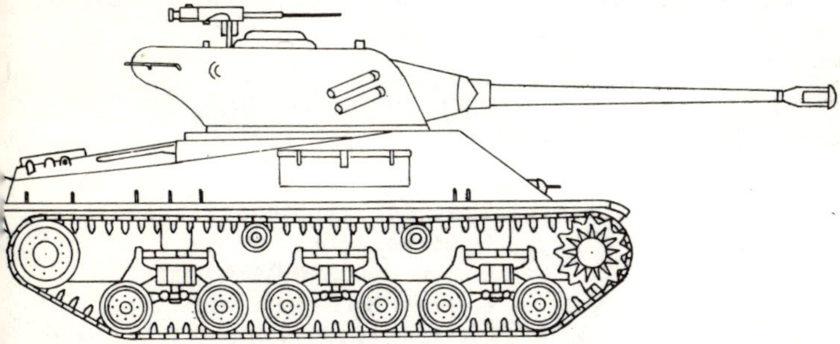

he American/Israeli M4 "Super Sherman" medium tank
Veight: 32 tons. *Crew:* 5. *Armament:* one 75-mm gun, plus one .5-inch and one
3-inch Browning machine gun. *Armour:* hull front 64-mm, sides and rear 38-mm,
ecking 19-mm, and belly 25-mm; turret front and sides 64-mm, and roof 25-mm.
ngine: one Ford GAA inline, 450-hp. *Speed:* 30 mph. *Range:* 100 miles. *Length:*
7 feet 6 inches. *Width:* 8 feet 9 inches. *Height:* 11 feet 3 inches.

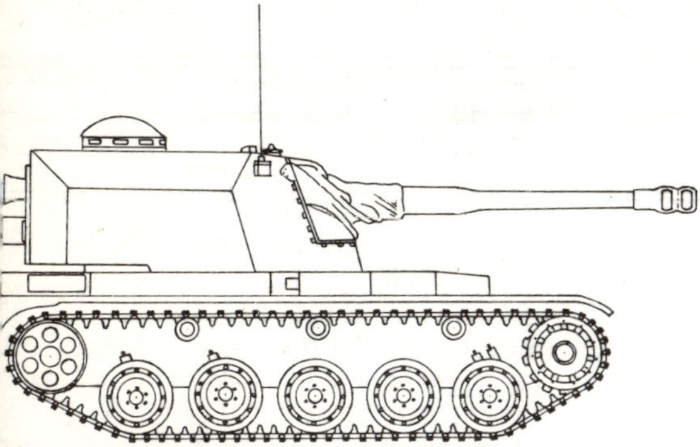

he French self-propelled 105-mm howitzer, AMX-13 chassis
/eight: 16.8 tons. *Crew:* 5. *Armament:* one 105-mm howitzer with 80 rounds, and
ne or two 7.5- or 7.62-mm AAT machine guns with 3,600 rounds. *Armour:* hull sides
9-mm, front and rear 15-mm; turret front and sides 13-mm. *Engine:* one SOFAM
Gxb inline, 240-hp. *Speed:* 40 mph. *Range:* 210 miles. *Length:* 16 feet 10 inches.
/idth: 8 feet 3 inches. *Height:* 8 feet 10 inches.

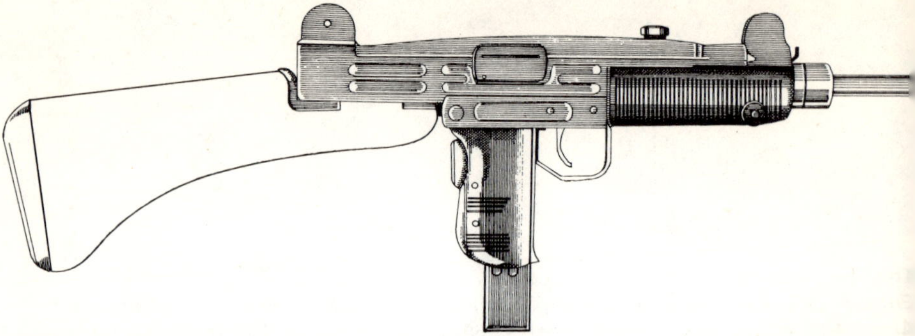

The Israeli Uzi sub-machine gun
Calibre: 9-mm parabellum. *Operation:* blowback, selective fire. *Weight:* 8.8 lbs. *Length:* 25.2 inches. *Barrel length:* 10.2 inches. *Feed:* 25, 32, or 40-round detachable staggered row box magazine. *Muzzle velocity:* 1,310 feet per second. *Cyclic rate of fire:* 650 rounds per minute.

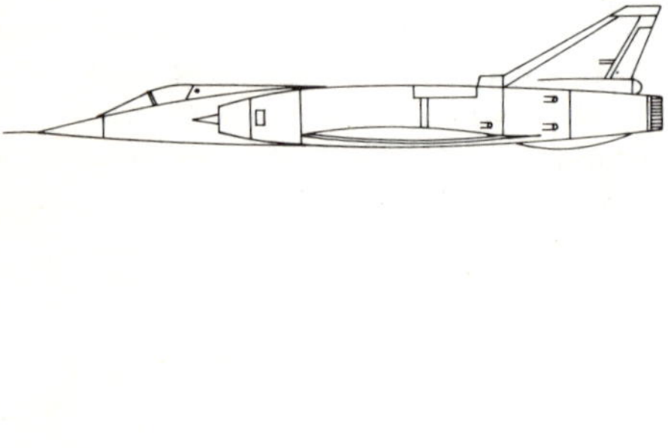

The French Dassault Mirage 111C fighter-bomber
Engine: one SNECMA Atar 09B3 turbojet, 13,225-lbs static thrust with afterburner. *Armament:* two 30-mm DEFA cannon, plus Matra R.511 or R.53 air-to-air missiles, Sidewinder air-to-ai missiles, Nord AS.30 air-to-ground missiles, 4,000-lbs of bombs, or napalm tanks. *Speed:* 1,430 mph at 36,000 feet (mach 2.15). *Ceiling:* 65,600 feet. *Radius:* 745 miles. *Weight empty/loaded:* 13,040/26,015 lbs. *Span:* 26 feet 11¾ inches. *Length:* 48 feet 5¼ inches. *Height:* 13 feet 11½ inches.

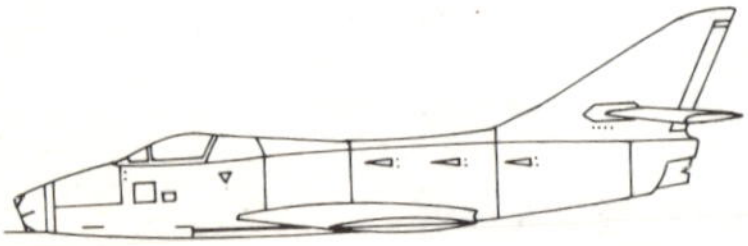

The French Dassault Super Mystère B-2 fighter
Engine: one SNECMA Atar 101G1 turbojet, 9,700-lbs static thrust. *Armament:* two 30-mm cannon, plus a under-fuselage pack of 55 air-to-air missiles and under-wing points for twc 1,100-lb bombs or 38 air-to-air missiles *Speed:* 743 mph at 38,000 feet. *Ceiling:* 55,750 feet. *Range:* 730 miles. *Weight loaded:* 22,050 lbs. *Span:* 34 feet 6¼ inches. *Length:* 46 feet 1 inch *Height:* 14 feet 11 inches.

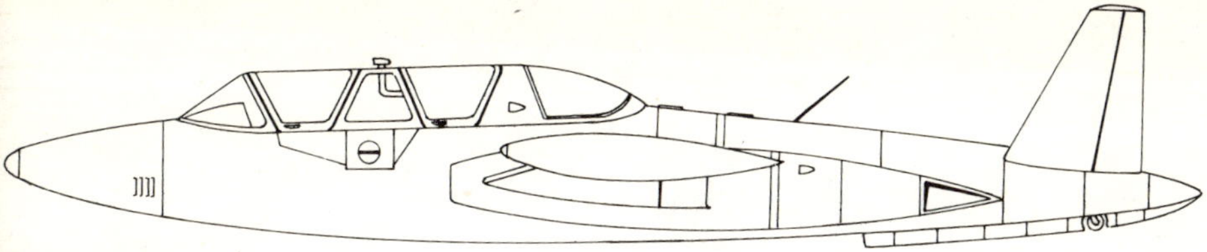

The French Potez (Air Fouga) Magister ground attack aircraft
Engines: two Turbomeca Marbore IIA turbojets, 880-lbs static thrust each. *Armament:* two 7.5- or 7.62-mm guns, plus two 110-lb bombs, two AS.11 anti-tank missiles, or two Matra 37- or 68-mm rocket packs. *Speed:* 440 mph. *Ceiling:* 36,000 feet. *Range:* 735 miles. *Weight loaded:* 7,055 lbs. *Span:* 39 feet 10 inches. *Length:* 33 feet. *Height:* 9 feet 2 inches.

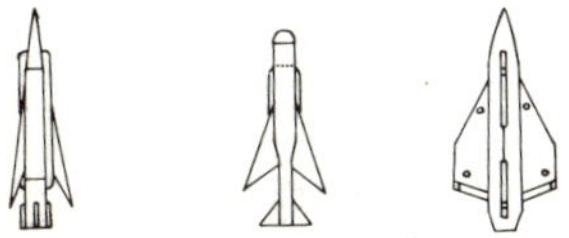

The French Matra R.530 air-to-air missile
Engine: one Hotchkiss-Brandt two-stage solid propellant rocket, 18,740-lbs thrust. *Warhead:* 60-lb proximity-fused H.E. *Guidance:* semi-active radar or infra-red. *Speed:* mach 2.7. *Range:* 11 miles. *Span:* 3 feet $7\frac{1}{4}$ inches. *Body diameter:* $10\frac{1}{4}$ inches. *Length:* 10 feet $9\frac{1}{4}$ inches. *Weight:* 430 lbs.

The French Nord AS. 30 air-to-surface missile (left)
Engine: two-stage liquid propellant rocket. *Warhead:* 510-lb delay or non-delay fused H.E. *Guidance:* radio. *Speed:* 1,120 mph. *Range:* 7.5 miles. *Span:* 3 feet $3\frac{1}{2}$ inches. *Body diameter:* 1 foot $1\frac{1}{2}$ inches. *Length:* 12 feet 7 inches. *Weight:* 1,146 lbs.

The American Raytheon MIM-23A Hawk surface-to-air missile (right)
Engine: one Aerojet-General M22 E8 rocket. *Warhead:* H.E. *Guidance:* semi-active radar. *Speed:* mach 2.5. *Range:* 22 miles. *Span:* 3 feet 11.4 inches. *Body diameter:* 1 foot 2 inches. *Length:* 16 feet 6 inches. *Weight:* 1,295 lbs.

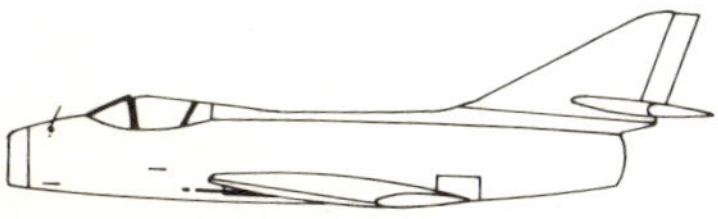

The French Dassault Mystère IVA fighter
Engine: one Hispano Suiza HS 250A turbojet, 6,280-lbs static thrust. *Armament:* four 20-mm cannon and 2,000 lbs of bombs or 16 rockets. *Speed:* 683 mph at sea level. *Ceiling:* 45,000 feet. *Range:* 820 miles. *Weight loaded:* 15,983 lbs. *Span:* 36 feet $5\frac{3}{4}$ inches. *Length:* 42 feet 2 inches. *Height:* 14 feet 5 inches.

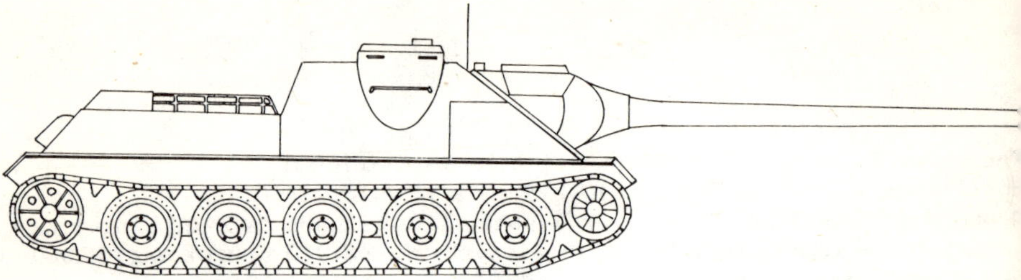

The Russian SU-100 tank destroyer
Weight: 31.6 tons. *Armament:* one 100-mm Model 1944 D-10S gun with 35 rounds. *Armour:* hull front 76-mm, sides and rear 45-mm. *Engine:* one V-2-34 diesel inline, 500-hp. *Speed:* 31 mph on roads and 25 mph cross-country. *Range:* 180 miles on roads (220 with additional fuel tanks) and 130 (210) cross-country. *Length:* 32 feet 10 inches. *Width:* 9 feet 10 inches. *Height:* 8 feet 4 inches. *Crew:* 4.

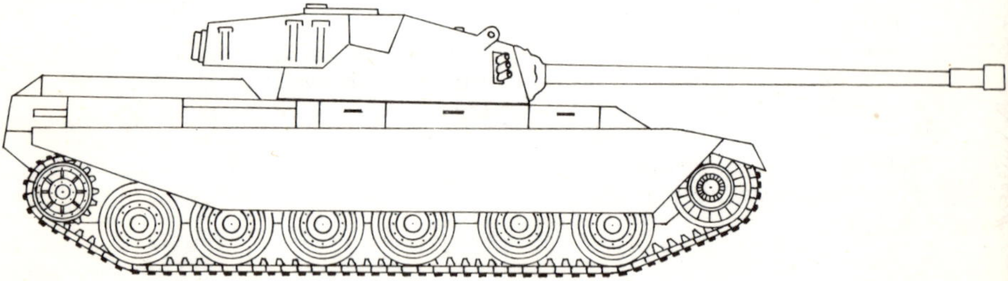

The British Centurion 3 medium tank
Weight: 49.5 tons. *Crew:* 4. *Armament:* one 83.4-mm (20-pounder) gun with 65 rounds, and one 7.92-mm Besa and one .3-inch Browning machine gun with 4,250 rounds. *Armour:* 76-mm maximum. *Engine:* one Rolls-Royce Meteor IVB inline, 650-hp. *Speed:* 21.5 mph. *Range:* 60 miles (without extra fuel tanks). *Length:* 32 feet 3 inches. *Width:* 11 feet 11½ inches. *Height:* 9 feet 7¾ inches.

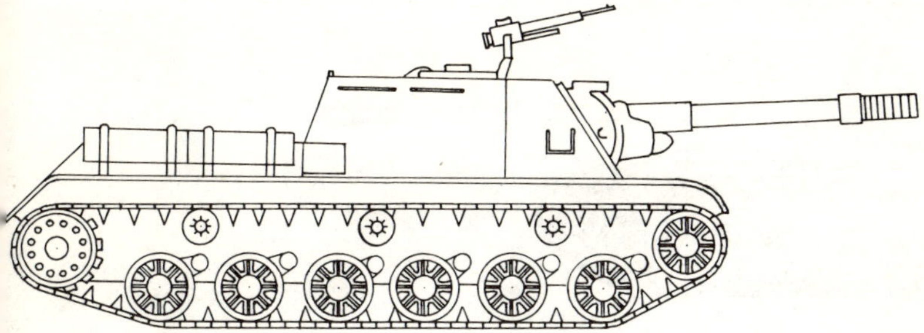

The Russian JSU-152 assault gun
Weight: 50 tons. *Armament:* one 152-mm Model 1943 ML 20S gun/howitzer with 20 rounds and one 12.7-mm Degtyarev machine gun. *Armour:* upper nose 110-mm, lower nose 127-mm, glacis plate 75-mm, upper sides 89-mm, lower sides 75-mm, rear 64-mm, decking 25-mm, and belly 19-mm. *Engine:* one Model V-2-1S diesel inline, 520-hp. *Speed:* 23 mph on roads and 10 mph cross-country. *Range:* 112 miles on roads (190 with additional tanks) and 52 miles cross-country. *Length:* 33 feet. *Width:* 10 feet 2 inches. *Height:* 8 feet 3 inches.

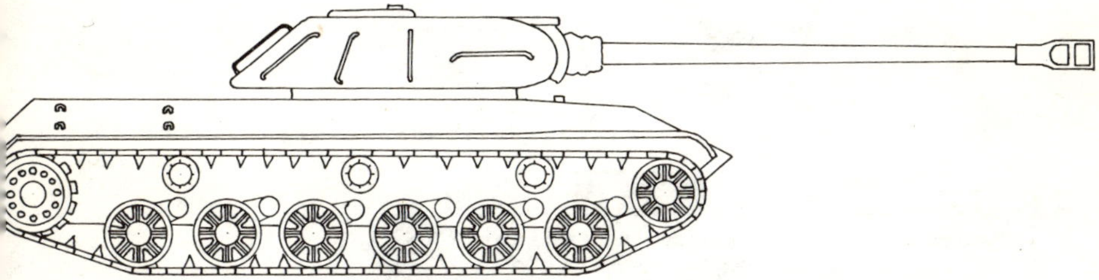

The Russian JS-3 heavy tank
Weight: 45.8 tons. *Crew:* 4. *Armament:* one 122-mm Model 1943 D-25 gun with 28 rounds, plus one 12.7-mm DShK and two 7.62-mm DT machine guns with 945 and 1,000 rounds respectively. *Armour:* hull front 120-mm, sides and rear 60- to 90-mm, decking 45-mm, and belly 35-mm; turret front 230-mm, roof 25-mm. *Engine:* one V-2-1S diesel inline, 513-hp. *Speed:* 23 mph on roads and 12 mph cross-country. *Range*: 130 miles on roads and 94 miles cross-country. *Length*: 32 feet 9 inches. *Width:* 10 feet 6 inches. *Height:* 8 feet 10¾ inches.

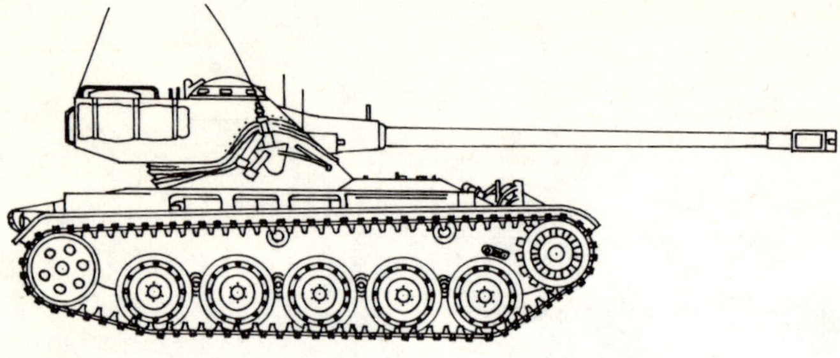

The French AMX-13 light tank
Weight: 14.8 tons. *Crew:* 3. *Armament:* one 75-mm gun in an F1-10 oscillating turret with 37 rounds, and one or two 7-5- or 7.62-mm AAT machine guns with 3,600 rounds. *Armour:* hull sides 19-mm, front and rear 15-mm; turrent front and sides 25-mm. *Engine:* one SOFAM 8 Gxb inline, 240-hp. *Speed:* 40 mph. *Range:* 210 miles. *Length:* 20 feet 9 inches. *Width:* 8 feet 3 inches. *Height:* 7 feet 4¼ inches.

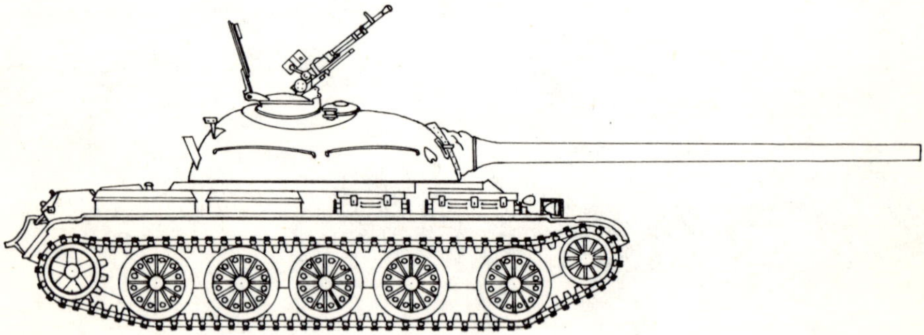

The Russian T-54 medium tank
Weight: 36 tons. *Armament:* one 100-mm Model 1944 D-10T gun with 34 rounds, plus one 12.7-mm DShK and one 7.62-mm machine gun with 500 and 3,000 rounds respectively. *Armour:* hull front 100-mm, sides 80-mm, decking 20-mm, and belly 30-mm; turret 30- to 210-mm. *Engine:* one V-54G diesel inline, 520-hp. *Speed:* 30 mph on roads and 16 mph cross-country. *Range:* 385 miles on roads and 270 miles. *Length:* 29 feet 7 inches. *Width:* 10 feet 9 inches. *Height:* 7 feet 10 inches.

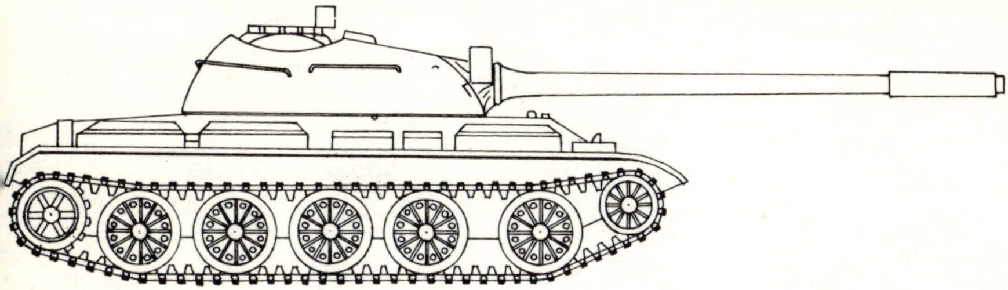

The Russian T-55 medium tank
Weight: **35 tons.** ***Crew:*** **4.** ***Armament:*** **one 100-mm D-10T2S gun with 43 rounds and one 7.62-mm DT machine gun with 2,200 rounds.** ***Armour:*** **hull front 100-mm, sides 80-mm, decking 30-mm, and belly 20-mm; turret 30- to 210-mm.** ***Engine:*** **one V-2-55 diesel inline, 580-hp.** ***Speed:*** **34.4 mph on roads and 20 mph cross-country.** ***Range:*** **220 miles on roads (477 with additional tanks) and 185 miles (430) cross-country.** ***Length:*** **27 feet 11½ inches.** ***Width:*** **10 feet 9 inches.** ***Height:*** **7 feet 10 inches.**

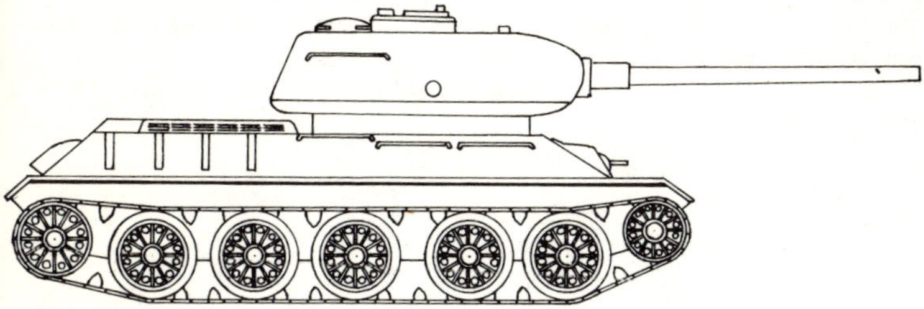

The Russian T-34/85 medium tank
Weight: **32 tons.** ***Crew:*** **5.** ***Armament:*** **one 85-mm Model 1944 ZIS-S-55 gun with 56 rounds and two 7.62-mm Degtyarev machine guns with 2,745 rounds.** ***Armour:*** **hull glacis, nose, sides, and rear 47-mm, roof 30-mm, and belly 20-mm; turret front and mantlet 100-mm, sides 85-mm, rear 75-mm, and roof 20-mm.** ***Engine:*** **one V-2-34 diesel inline, 500-hp.** ***Speed:*** **32 mph.** ***Range:*** **220 miles.** ***Length:*** **24 feet 9 inches.** ***Width:*** **9 feet 10 inches.** ***Height:*** **7 feet 11 inches.**

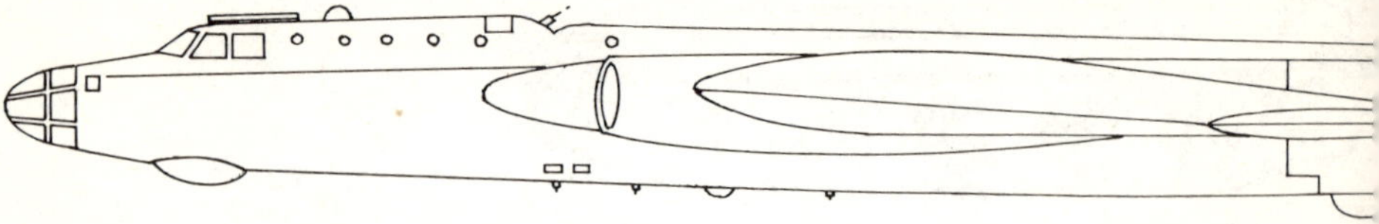

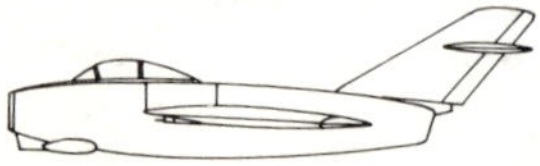

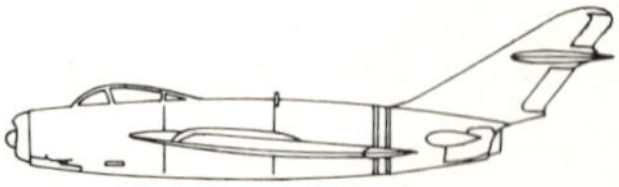

The Russian Mikoyan-Gurevich MiG-15 "Fagot-B" fighter-bomber
Engine: one Klimov VK-1A turbojet, 6,990-lbs static thrust at sea level. *Armament:* one 37-mm N cannon with 40 rounds and two 23-mm NS cannon with 80 rounds each, plus up to 1,100 lbs of bombs or rockets. *Speed:* 684 mph. *Initial climb:* 10,400 feet per minute. *Ceiling:* 51,000 feet. *Range:* 560 miles. *Weight loaded:* 11,085 lbs. *Span:* 33 feet 1 inch. *Length:* 36 feet 3¼ inches. *Height:* 11 feet 1¾ inches.

The Russian Mikoyan-Gurevich MiG-17 "Fresco-C" fighter-bomber
Engine: one Klimov VK-1A turbojet, 6,990-lbs static thrust at sea level. *Armament:* one 37-mm NS-2 cannon and two 23-mm NR VYa cannon, plus up to 1,100 lbs of bombs or 32 55-mm rockets. *Speed:* 725 mph at sea level. *Ceiling:* 57,500 feet. *Range:* 700 miles. *Weight loaded:* 14,750 lbs. *Span:* 31 feet. *Length:* 36 feet 3 inches. *Height:* 11 feet.

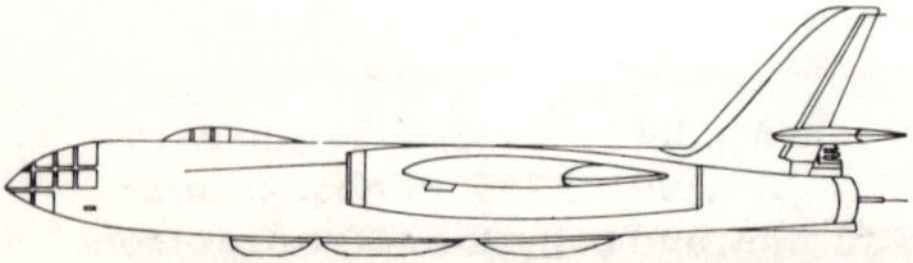

The Russian Ilyushin I1-28 "Beagle" bomber
Engines: two Klimov VK-1 turbojets, 5,950-lbs static thrust each. *Armament:* two 23-mm NS-23 and two 20-mm cannons, plus up to 6,500 lbs of bombs. *Speed:* 580 mph at 19,680 feet. *Ceiling:* 41,000 feet. *Radius:* 850 miles. *Weight loaded:* 43,000 lbs. *Span:* 64 feet 5¾ inches. *Length:* 58 feet 1½ inches. *Height:* 22 feet.

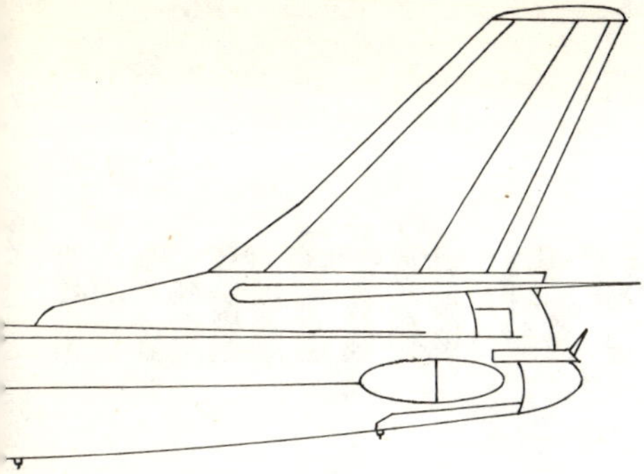

The Russian Tupolev Tu-16 "Badger" bomber
Engines: two Mikulin AM-3M turbojets, 20,950-lbs static thrust each at sea level. *Armament:* nine 23-mm cannon and up to 19,800 lbs of bombs. *Speed:* 587 mph at 35,000 feet. *Ceiling:* 42,650 feet. *Range:* 3,975 miles. *Weight loaded:* 175,000 lbs. *Span:* 110 feet. *Length:* 120 feet. *Height:* 35 feet 6 inches.

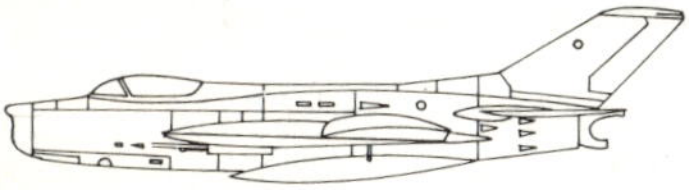

The Russian Mikoyan-Gurevich MiG-19 "Farmer-C" fighter
Engines: two Mikulin AM-9b turbojets, 7,150-lbs static thrust each with afterburning. *Armament:* three 30-mm cannon. *Speed:* 860 mph at 36,000 feet/mach 1.3 at 20,000 feet. *Ceiling:* 55,000 feet. *Range:* 850 miles. *Weight loaded:* 19,840 lbs. *Span:* 32 feet. *Length:* 37 feet 6 inches.

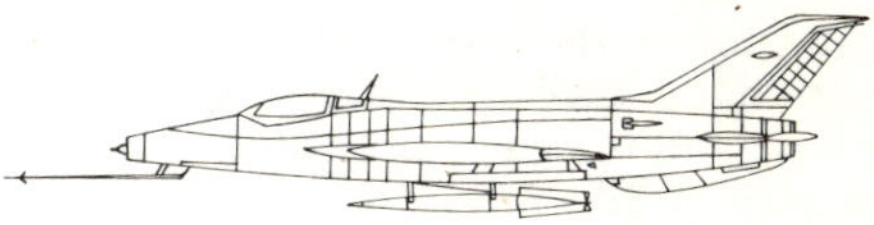

The Russian Mikoyan-Gurevich MiG-21 "Fishbed-C" fighter
Engine: one Tumansky RD-11 turbojet, 12,500-lbs static thrust with afterburner. *Armament:* two 30-mm cannon and two "Atoll" air-to-air missiles or 16 55-mm rockets. *Speed:* 1,320 mph at 36,000 feet (mach 2). *Climb:* 30,000 feet per minute initially. *Ceiling:* 65,600+ feet. *Radius:* 350 miles. *Weight empty/loaded:* 12,100/17,000 lbs. *Span:* 23 feet 5½ inches. *Length:* 51 feet 8½ inches (including nose boom).

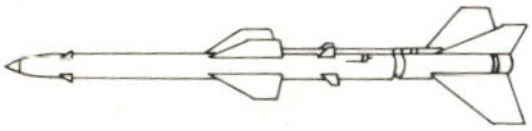

The Russian V750VK (SAM-2 "Guideline") surface-to-air missile
Engine: liquid propellant sustainer with solid propellant booster. *Warhead:* 288-lb contact, proximity, or command detonated H.E. warhead. *Guidance:* radio. *Speed:* mach 3.5. *Range:* 25 miles. *Span:* 5 feet 7 inches. *Body diameter:* 2 feet 2 inches (booster) and 1 foot 8 inches (2nd stage). *Length:* 34 feet 9 inches. *Weight:* 5,000 lbs.

The Egyptian Al Kahir surface-to-surface missile.
Details of this weapon are impossible to obtain, but it has a range of some 375 miles, is 39.4 feet long and 3.94 feet in diameter. The warhead is probably in the region of 1,300 pounds.

Israel's 'pre-emptive attack'

What was to go down in history as the Six-Day War began early in the morning of Monday 5th June. It was virtually won by Israel before noon that day, but before it ended, six days later, there was much hard fighting and thousands of lives were lost.

Perhaps nobody will ever really know who fired the first shot. Nasser, in welcoming Iraq to the UAR and Jordanian alliance the night before, had proclaimed: 'We are eager for battle in order to force the enemy to awake from his dreams and meet Arab reality face to face.' In the event air raid sirens screamed in Tel Aviv and at 7.45am the Israeli radio announced that an Egyptian column was rolling towards the Negev and Egyptian planes heading for Israel had been picked up on Israel's early warning radar. Few people regarded this information as other than a rationalisation. A tiny country like Israel could not possibly fight a defensive war; only pre-emptive action could make sense to those responsible for preventing disaster overtaking their country. Defence against an attack from the air was difficult, because the country was too small for any early warning system to give sufficient time for Israeli fighters to scramble. Cairo was twenty-five minutes flying time from Tel Aviv, but Tel Aviv was only four-and-a-half

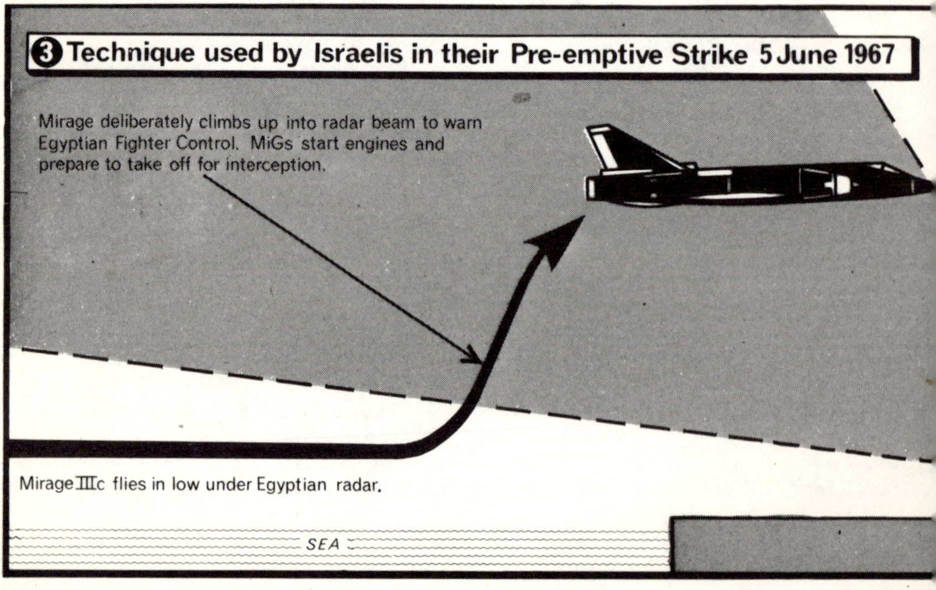

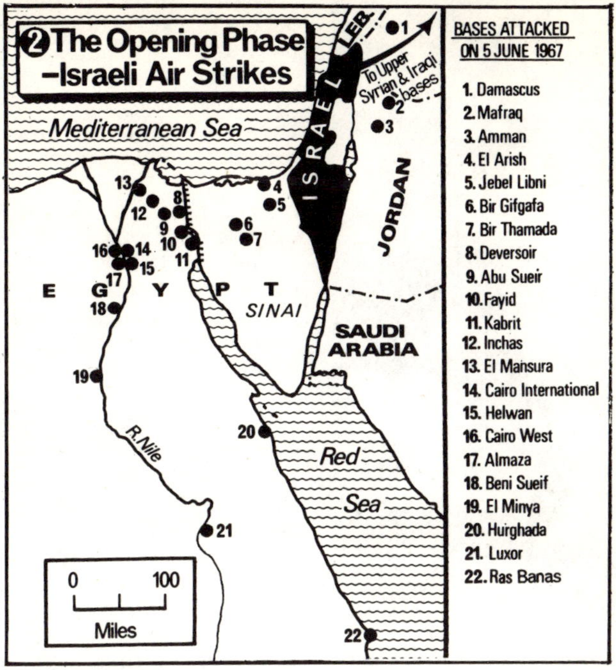

minutes flying distance from the forward Egyptian air base at El Arish. Anti-aircraft guns were not effective against fast, high-flying jet bombers targeting on populated areas, and the few ground-to-air missiles which Israel had been able to afford were sufficient only to give a limited protection to Tel Aviv, and the Israeli nuclear installation in the Negev.

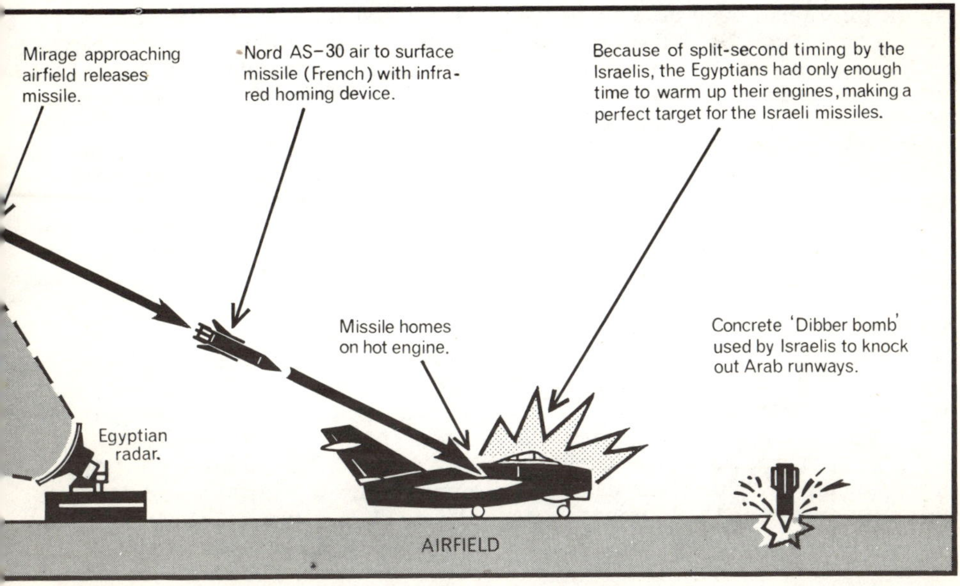

Field-Marshal Amer

For this reason therefore, the Israeli Air Force had prepared and trained for an offensive role designed to obliterate the enemy's air forces. In uninhabited parts of the Negev the Israeli pilots had been practicing low flying, precision bombing and the shooting up of model ground targets which bore a distinct resemblance to the Egyptian airfields. At the same time the ground crews had been training in the rapid refuelling, servicing, and turn-round of the aircraft. Thus, when the day came, every pilot was supremely confident in his ability to destroy his target, and all the ground crews were equally confident in their ability to keep the aircraft flying.

The Israeli Air Force went into action at 7.45am (8.45am Cairo time). The target was ten Egyptian airfields, and the plan was to strike them all simultaneously. The time had been shrewdly chosen as the moment when the Egyptians would be least expecting an attack. Visibility would be good, and the customary dawn stand-to, during which airborne MiGs would be waiting to pounce on intruders, was over. Most of the Egyptian pilots would be having their breakfast and their commanders would not yet have reached their offices. Furthermore the Israeli pilots, who had a long day ahead, would be able to get a good night's rest.

One additional advantage which came as a welcome bonus was unplanned, unanticipated and unexpected. Two of the key Egyptian commanders were caught literally up in the air. Field-Marshal Ali Amer, the UAR commander-in-chief, and his air force commander, General Mahmoud Sidky, were in an aircraft flying from Cairo to inspect Egyptian troops in Sinai when the Israeli fighter-bombers screamed in to their targets. As a safety measure the Egyptian anti-aircraft batteries had been given orders not to fire on any aircraft over Sinai while Amer's Ilyushin was airborne. The latter could not land in Sinai because all the airfields were under attack, and ultimately had to return to Cairo. For ninety vital minutes the two key UAR commanders were out of touch with their forces and unable to give orders. To make matters worse the senior Egyptian field commanders in Sinai had left their posts to go to Thamed to greet Amer.

As the Israeli planners had hoped, the attack came as a complete surprise to the Egyptians – 'an hour earlier than anticipated' – as Radio Cairo ruefully put it. The Israeli pilots had nine objectives in all: the airfields at El Arish, Jebel Libni, Bir Gifgafa and Bir Thamada in the Sinai; Fayid and Kabrit on the Suez Canal; Abu Sueir and Cairo West in the Delta area; and Beni Sueif about sixty miles south of Cairo. With the exception of Fayid, which the Israeli pilots took some time to find because it was shrouded in mist, all these airfields were hit within fifteen minutes of the scheduled time. The attacking planes

An Egyptian airfield comes under attack from Israeli planes

flew in low to avoid detection and only as they approached their targets did they climb and suddenly become visible on the Egyptian radar screens. The final climb was a deliberate ruse to give the Egyptians a belated warning and so induce their pilots to attempt a scramble. Caught on the runways or in the cockpits of their machines they would then be destroyed with their aircraft.

Approaching their targets under cover of an air umbrella of about forty Mirage fighters, the first waves of Israeli Mystères met virtually no opposition. Because of their orders about Amer the Egyptian anti-aircraft gunners held their fire, and the only Egyptian aircraft airborne at the time of the initial strike were four unarmed training planes which were promptly shot down. Subsequent waves of attackers, which arrived over the targets as previous flights flew back to refuel and re-arm, prior to another attack, ran into slightly more opposition – mostly from the AA guns which came into action when their crews realized what was happening. Only eight MiGs managed to take off during the action and at the cost of two Israeli Mirages, these were all brought down. The Israeli aircraft spent no more than ten minutes over their targets; this allowed them to make three or four attacks before their ammunition and bombs were expended, and fuel limitations compelled the pilots to turn back. During the initial sorties the runways and aircraft parking areas were strafed with cannon fire, and the Mirages' bombs were dropped on the runways during the final attack. Attack followed attack in successive waves – each consisting of about forty planes – as the Israeli flights followed one another at ten-minute intervals. As one assault lifted, the planes of the following wave flew in to the target, the next was on its way, the fourth

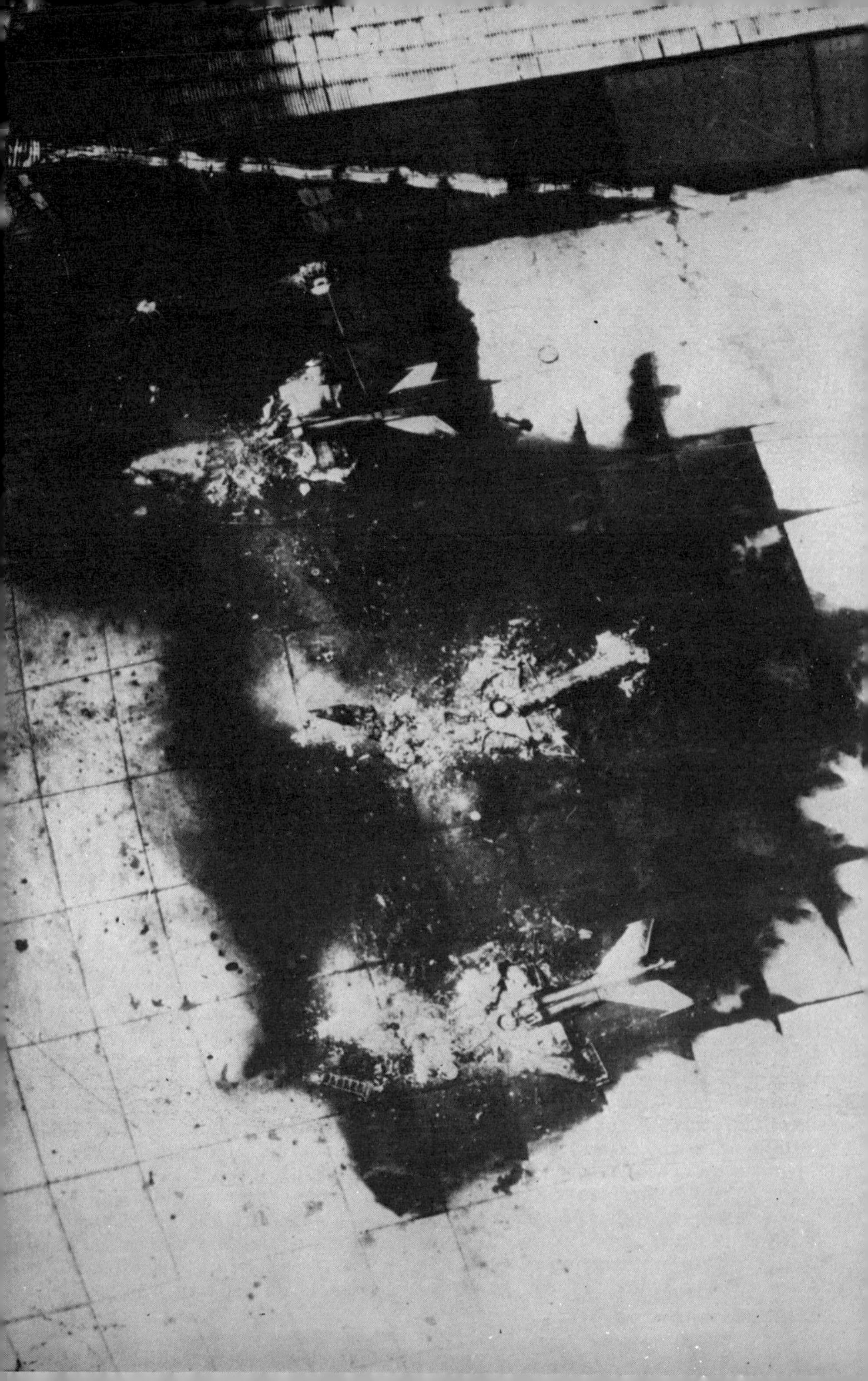

was preparing to take off, and the ground crews were waiting to refuel, re-arm and turn the returning aircraft of the first wave. Within fifty minutes the first wave was back over the same targets, and a pattern of successive and continuous attack on the Egyptian airfields was maintained until noon – by which time Nasser's air force had been practically wiped out. Then, after a short interval, the same Israeli planes took off again to attack the Egyptian airports further afield. The Ilyushin carrying Field-Marshal Amer and General Sidky had to stay in the air for an hour-and-a-half until it eventually managed to land at Cairo International Airport. Seventeen major airfields were attacked and in just under three hours nearly 300 planes of the Egyptian Air Force were destroyed. These included thirty Tupolev-16 heavy bombers, twenty-seven Ilyushin medium bombers,

Three MiG21s lie shattered after the Israeli attack on the morning of 5th June

A MiG19 destroyed on the ground

seventy MiG-19 fighters, twelve Sukhoi-7 fighter bombers, ninety MiG-21 fighters and thirty-two transport planes and helicopters.

The surprise on which the Israelis had gambled was utterly complete. At nearly every UAR airfield the Egyptian aircraft were trapped on their parking aprons – wingtip to wingtip – and no attempt had been made at dispersion or camouflage. This, said the Arabs later – and Soviet spokesmen in Moscow angily concurred – was a clear indication that Israel had struck the first blow. In Cairo the saddest remark that was heard during the war was: Trust those Jews to attack when they knew all our pilots would be having breakfast.'

To the Arabs the devastating power of the Israeli attack was as stunning as the surprise with which it took place. The majority of the Egyptian aircraft were destroyed by incredibly

A SAM-2 missile supplied by the Soviet Union to the Egyptian ground defences, pictured after its capture intact by Israeli forces

accurate cannon fire, and the airfields were put out of action by bombing which disrupted the runways. Most of these bombs were conventional 250lb, 500lb and 100lb types, but some of those dropped on the airfields west of the Suez Canal had been developed for the express purpose of cracking the hard surface of concrete runways. (None were dropped on the Sinai airfields, which the Israelis hoped to capture for use by their own planes). When one of these bombs struck the ground, booster rockets drove its 365lb warhead down into the hard surface, while delayed-action fuzes made the moment of detonation uncertain. Known now as concrete 'dibber' bombs, they were new to the Egyptians, and the Israeli success was partially attributed to the use of this 'secret' weapon. In the first few minutes of the early attacks the ground crews and Egyptian soldiers gallantly tried to repair the damaged runways and put out fires and salvage aircraft which had not been hit. But continual explosions of delayed action 'dibbers' and Israeli cannon fire eventually compelled them to give up. Once they had recovered from their initial surprise, the Egyptian anti-aircraft gunners fought back hard,

A SAM-2 missile site in the desert

and it was they who accounted for most of the planes which the Israelis lost. A number of the much-vaunted Soviet SAM-2 air defence missiles were released against the attacking Israeli aircraft during the course of the day. But the Israelis flew too low and too fast for them, and none of the missiles scored a hit. Slow to get off their launching pads and slow to accelerate, the performance of the SAM-2s was demonstrably less effective than that of the AA guns.

By noon on the first day of the war rumours that their air force had destroyed about 200 Egyptian aircraft were circulating among the Israelis. But no confirmation was forthcoming from official quarters, and on General Dayan's orders the rumours were deliberately played down. 'Let the Arabs do all the talking,' Dayan told the Israeli government spokesman. He had guessed that Nasser's generals would be reluctant to tell their chief of the Egyptian losses, and that when Nasser did learn their magnitude there would be a demand for UN intervention or a ceasefire to stave off further disaster and prevent the Israelis from exploiting their success. Dayan was also apprehensive of Soviet reaction when Moscow learned

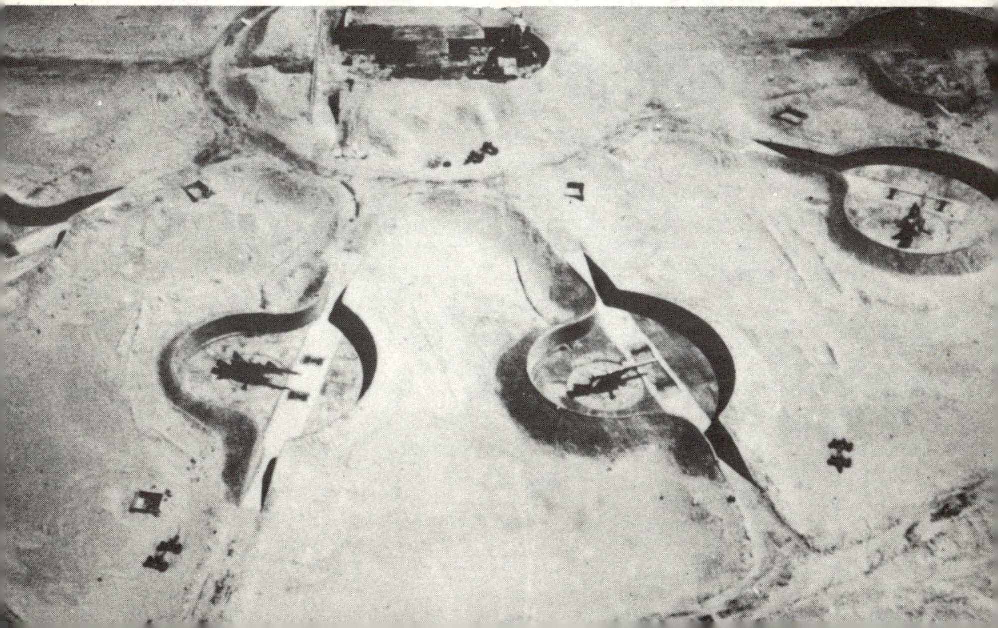

that many of the aircraft and other war materials supplied to Egypt had been destroyed. Thus, until the true facts were revealed at an Israeli press conference on the morning of the second day (6th June), Arab bulletins teeming with false claims of Israeli planes shot down, were retransmitted without comment by the Israeli Broadcasting Service. In Cairo each fresh bit of wishful reporting was jubilantly received by people gathered round transistor radios at street corners, and mobs of students chanted 'We shall fight, we shall fight, our beloved Nasser, we are behind you to Tel Aviv!' One report from Radio Cairo told of an Israeli pilot whose plane had been shot down near Zagazig in the Nile delta. Landing by parachute, he had been seized by the local fellahin who had chopped him to pieces with the axes they used in the fields.

Whilst such news kept the Arabs in optimistic darkness, the Israelis – who could also listen in to Radio Cairo, and many of whom could understand Arabic – were naturally anxious. To some extent their fears were soothed by a statement put out by Brigadier Chaim Hertzog, the chief military commentator, who condemned the Egyptian claims as 'premature, unclear and utterly unauthorized.' And there can be little doubt that the Israeli policy of refusing to lift the fog of war for the benefit of their enemies did pay off. Nasser himself did not learn of the full extent of the Israeli blow until some six or seven hours later, and with the Egyptian High Command was slow to appreciate its significance for the air battle. When Nasser welcomed Jordan's entry into the war that morning he thought he still had an air force. When he learned the truth he tried to explain it away by accusing the US and Britain of having shared in the attack.

King Hussein decides to commit Jordan in the war. Here he is pictured inspecting army positions a few days before the war

In Tel Aviv the unfamiliar wail of air raid sirens shortly before 8am was the first indication that the war had started. But no amount of warning, however shrill, ever quite prepares a people for an event of this nature; people were reluctant to take shelter and the morning bustle of Tel Aviv was scarcely disturbed. The same sort of attitude was prevalent in Jerusalem and other places, and it was not until about 9am when both Israeli and Arab radios announced the opening of hostilities that the mood changed. Many inhabitants then scrambled for places in the air raid shelters, where many of them slept for the next three or four nights. In Tel Aviv the warning siren screamed twelve times during the first day – the longest alert being at noon when Jordan started to shell the city.

Throughout the crisis the Israelis had been hoping that Jordan would stay out of the war, and frantic messages had been sent to King Hussein through local agencies of the United Nations asking him to hold his fire. If he would keep his peace, so too would they, the Israelis said. But Hussein, the most moderate of the Arab rulers, had gone too far to be able to back down now; he was trapped by his commitments to the rest of the Arab world. At 9am a message was received from Field-Marshal Amer informing Hussein that the war with Israel had begun and urging Jordan to commence hostilities immediately in accordance with the pact signed in Cairo. In attacks against the UAR airfields 75 per cent of the Israeli air force had been destroyed, the message continued. This, of course, was complete fabrication, as was the claim that Egyptian aircraft were now attacking Israel. But any doubts which Hussein might have had at this time were quickly dispelled by what appeared to be confirmation of Amer's statement from a Jordanian source, when what were identified as a large number of aircraft flying from Egypt towards Israel were picked up by Jordan's radar stations. (These were Israeli planes, in fact, returning to base after their first sorties.) So Hussein decided to act, and at 9.30am Israeli hopes that Jordan would stay out of the fray were shattered. Broadcasting over Radio Amman, the king called on his people to join in the *jihad;* Jordan had been attacked, he said, the Jordanian army and air force had been placed under the command of General Riad, and 'the hour of revenge' had come. The Israelis were surprised, but many were not dismayed – for if the war with Egypt was long prepared, action against Jordan was opportunity itself. To fight for the holy city of Jerusalem was the chance to fulfil Jewish prophecy.

Following King Hussein's broadcast, the Jordanians were expected to attack in conjunction with Syria and Iraq. Confusion attributable to a spurious message – purporting to come from Field-Marshal Amer, but originated by Israeli Intelligence – and a message from the Syrians which said that they had been caught unawares by the suddenness of the outbreak of hostilities, inevitably caused delay. The Syrians said that their force was not yet ready to strike Israel. No doubt they were hoping that Hussein's planes would be destroyed by the Israelis before they committed their own to battle. To the Syrians Hussein was still the 'Tom Thumb Tyrant', and they had a sharp eye to a settlement of differences with Jordan when the war with Israel was over. The Iraqis were also slow to respond to the holy war call. But at 11am a signal to Hussein stated that Iraqi aircraft had already taken off to bomb targets in Israel. Subsequently the Iraqis claimed to have raided Tel Aviv and to have destroyed 'seven aircraft on an Israeli airfield.' Neither the initial statement nor the claim which followed were true. Throughout the war Iraqi air activity was confined to a single sneak attack by a solitary TU-16 which dropped a few bombs on Nathanya. So far as Hussein was concerned, however, there was no reason to suppose that the Syrian and Iraqi messages were not authentic and he ordered his aircraft to attack Israel. Sixteen of Jordan's twenty-two Hawker Hunters took off to bomb the airfields at Nathanya, Kfar Sirkin, Kfar Sava and other targets. By about 11.30am all sixteen Hunters were back at their airfields, and their pilots reported they had destroyed four Israeli planes on the ground.

The Israelis' reaction was both prompt and devastating. Having dealt with the Egyptian air force, they turned their efforts to the elimination of that of Jordan. Shortly after noon two flights, each of four Mirages, took off to attack the Jordanian air bases at Mafraq and Amman. There they caught the Hunters refuelling and rearming after their bombing mission over Israel. When the Mirages turned for home eighteen Hunters were left blazing, destroyed beyond repair; and bombs had disrupted the runways. To round off their mission the Mirages then attacked and shot up what appeared to be suitable targets encountered on the return journey. Such targets ranged from moving vehicles to – according to the Jordanians – King Hussein's palace. In the course of the raid one Mirage was hit by Jordanian anti-aircraft gunners, but the pilot managed to bail out over the Sea of Galilee, where he was picked up by an Israeli patrol boat.

In one short raid the Israelis had crippled the Jordanian air force which was now left literally without planes. Most of the pilots escaped death, and Hussein packed them off to Iraq where they spent the rest of the war flying Iraqi Hunters. Worse was to come, and Hussein claimed later that if the Syrians had carried out their part of the Arab pact and struck at Israel when they were called upon to do so his planes would have been airborne sooner. Then they might well have caught the Israeli aircraft returning from their raids against Egypt – airborne but short of ammunition and fuel, or on the ground refuelling – and, by destroying them, blunted the weapon which gave the Israelis ultimate victory. Maybe this could have been so; since the Hawker Hunter is reputedly more manoeuvrable than the Mystère and Mirage. But history abounds with ifs and might-have-beens, and it seems unlikely that anything the Jordanians could have done would have affected the ultimate result.

The Syrian air force was struck and paralysed about the same time as that of Jordan. At 12.15pm sixteen Mystères attacked the four main airfields south of Damascus. After twenty minutes of bombing and strafing, a blazing mess of wrecked Syrian aircraft and cratered runways testified to the swift vengeance of the Israelis which Radio Damascus had that morning rashly promised would be 'destroyed within four days'. Schools in Damascus had been closed, more in celebration than precaution against air raids, and school children were now put to work filling sandbags to stack round public buildings. No air raid shelters had been prepared in the Syrian capital, and after this brief demonstration of Israeli air power the Syrians hastily converted a couple of discotheques. West of Damascus, the population of Beirut was also frantically taking some half-hearted precautions against air raids. Like other Arab states the Lebanon had also declared war on Israel, but apart from broadcasts containing the same mixture of exhilaration and invective as that from the other Arab radio networks, the Lebanese Government made no hostile move. The Lebanese Prime Minister Rashid Karame was keen to get in at the kill, but the army's chief of staff, General Bustani, knew that his country's armed forces were no match for those of Israel, and when on the Tuesday (the second day of the war) Rashid Karame ordered him to take the field, Bustani refused. The Prime Minister then ordered Bustani's arrest, but as no one would comply with this order either, nothing happened. Fortunately for the Lebanese this stalemate lasted long enough for the truth to overtake the wishful reporting that had set the tone of the first day's battle bulletin from Cairo. Karame, realizing his mistake, toned down his bellicosity and tried to forget that he had ever wanted to wage war against Israel. Apart from one clash between Israeli aircraft and two Lebanese Hunters over the Sea of Galilee the Lebanese stayed out of the war and the Israelis were content to leave them alone.

In the event neither the Syrians nor the Lebanese were disturbed by further air raids on the first day of the war. Except for one raid against the main Iraqi airfield, once the wings of the Syrian Air Force had been clipped and Hussein's air power pulverised, the Israelis turned their attention back to the major enemy, Egypt. The airfields which had been hit in the early raids were struck again, while a series of other attacks were concentrated on the Egyptian radar stations. By nightfall all the radar installations in Sinai as well as most of those in the Delta and Canal zones had been knocked out, and the Israeli air force could claim almost complete freedom of the skies. Apart from three or four isolated attacks by Egyptian MiGs on Israeli troops in the Sinai no Arab aircraft ventured anywhere over Israel or attempted to intervene in the land battles after this. In contrast the Israelis gave massive aerial support to their ground forces, and flew at will whenever and wherever they wished – making frequent flights over Cairo and the Delta area, parts of Iraq, Syria and Jordan, as well as all over Sinai before it was overrun. On occasions the Arabs attempted to resist the incursions into their air space. But SAM missiles fired at the intruders proved to be as ineffective as they had been on the first day of the war, and the Israelis quickly got the measure of the anti-aircraft gunners. On a number of occasions dog fights developed when Egyptian MiGs and Iraqi Hunters intercepted Israeli aircraft. After the war the Israelis claimed to have downed 61 Egyptian aircraft and 16 other Arab planes in aerial combat. The cost in terms of Israeli planes is believed to have been about 40, although the Israelis have never confirmed or denied this figure. Thirteen Israeli pilots were taken prisoner – nine by the Egyptians, two by the Jordanians, and two by the Syrians; and five other Israeli pilots who had to bail out over enemy territory were killed on landing.

It was the pre-emptive attack by the Israeli air force which formed the key to their success in the land battles which were to follow. Possibly they would still have won the war without this massive air assault, but victory could have entailed many more Israeli casualties and it would have taken longer. Some of the Arab troops fought stubbornly – the Jordanians in particular. But absolute mastery of the air by the Israelis meant ultimate Arab defeat. Hussein, unaware of the extent of Egypt's losses, could not believe that the Israeli air force was capable of the sustained effort deployed against his Arab Legionnaires. Thus it was partially understandable that for a while, at least, he should support Nasser's claim that American and British aircraft had joined in Israel's attack.

How this canard originated is still shrouded in mystery. But it seems that when the truth about the destruction of the Egyptian air force could no longer be hidden from Nasser, the UAR High Command tried to explain it away by laying the blame on the United States and Britain. The accusation was fed by the prevailing bewilderment and confusion, and Nasser was desperate to find an excuse for the Arab debacle. By implicating the United States and Britain he probably hoped to persuade Moscow to come to his rescue. In effect there was never a chance of this ploy working. Russian ships monitoring air movement in the

Mediterranean knew from their own radar that no American or British planes were involved and the Soviet ambassador in Cairo went to Nasser and bluntly told him so. Nevertheless Nasser stuck to his claim and just before dawn on the morning of the second day the Israelis monitored and tape-recorded a radio-telephone conversation in which Hussein telephoned Nasser to say that 400 aircraft were attacking Jordan, and after some discussion both Arab leaders agreed, according to the taped dialogue released by the Israelis, to say that the United States and Britain were participating in the war. The vital passages were spoken by Nasser:

Nasser: Hello – will we say the US and England or just the US?

Hussein: The US and England.

Nasser: Does England have aircraft carriers?

Hussein: (Answer unintelligible).

Nasser: By God, I say that I will make an announcement and you will make an announcement, and we will see to it that the Syrians make an announcement that American and British planes are taking part against us from aircraft carriers. We will stress the matter and we will drive the point home . . .'

The United States and British governments promptly denied this allegation, and both countries asked the UN to send observers to the airfields and carriers from which air support for the Israelis was supposed to have been flown. None were sent and Hussein admitted later that the 'vast umbrella' over Jordan had been entirely Israeli. Nasser, however, stuck to his story, insisting that 'three times as many' planes as Israel possessed had attacked the Arab

Egyptian planes attack advancing Israeli troops near the Suez Canal

forces. This, combined with the fact that it was inconceivable to ordinary Egyptian opinion that little Israel could beat them without outside assistance, meant that the Arabs believed, and probably still continue to believe, that American and British aircraft were instrumental in forcing an Israeli victory.

The truth of course is different. That the pre-emptive strike on Egypt and consequent destruction of Arab airpower played the decisive part in deciding the outcome of the war, there is no denying. But the credit must go entirely to the Israelis, for their professionalism, careful planning, hard training and meticulous preparations.

War in Sinai

Sinai is a bare and hostile desert separating Africa from Asia, and the Mediterranean from the Indian Ocean. This is the wilderness where the children of Israel wandered for forty years before entering the Promised Land, and where the tablets recording the Ten Commandments were delivered to Moses. It is the gateway to Palestine from Egypt, or, seen the other way round, the gateway to Egypt from Israel. In normal circumstances the only inhabitants of this inhospitable strip of terrain are the nomadic bedouin roaming among its sifted dunes in search of scrub-grass for their goats. But armies have tramped across the sands of Sinai for centuries, and it is an ideal battleground for modern warfare, perfect tank country where the protagonists can clash without involving civilian populations. In 1956 this desert waste was the scene of the first battles between Egypt and Israel; in 1967 it was to be the scene of an even more momentous clash between those two nations.

At the end of May there were nearly 100,000 Egyptian soldiers and 1,000 tanks in Sinai: seven divisions, two of them armoured. Of these divisions, only the 20th Palestine Division stationed in the Gaza strip, and the 7th Infantry Division deployed along the Israeli border, had been there before the crisis. The other five divisions had been rushed across the Suez Canal when Nasser began his brinkmanship, and when hostilities commenced they were not ready. Most of the Egyptian officers did not really expect to have to fight; other crises had stopped short of war, and they were confident that Nasser's victory would be diplomatic and non-military. Consequently few of them were concerned about instant readiness. Communications and administrative facilities had not been properly organised, and although there were ample stocks of rations, fuel and ammunition in the Sinai supply dumps they had not been distributed. One of the causes of this operational and administrative confusion lay with the way in which the much publicized build-up was conducted. Division followed division into the forward areas, units were shuffled pointlessly from one location to another. Thus on the morning of 5th June it was estimated that about a quarter of the Egyptian

Israeli soldiers in the front line section in the Negev Desert

4 Egyptian Dispositions in Sinai
MEDITERRANEAN SEA
Port Said
20 Div
7 Inf Div
Beersheba
ISRAEL
SUEZ
2 Inf Div
3 Inf Div
4 Armd Div
CANAL
Shazli Force
Bir Thamada
Suez
6 Inf Div
JORDAN
Eilat
Aqaba
SINAI
Abu Zenima
EGYPT
Gulf of Suez
Gulf of Aqaba
SAUDI ARABIA
El Tur
Armd Bde
0
50
Miles
RED SEA

vehicles were non-runners because they had broken down or had no fuel.

The Egyptian High Command deployed their seven divisions both for offensive action and for defence. The 20th Palestine Division in the Gaza Strip had an almost rigid defensive role in that region, while the 7th Division sat in strongly fortified positions from Rafah to El Arish covering the coastal road across Sinai to Kantara. In the Abu Agheila area further south the 2nd Infantry Division blocked the central Sinai road to Ismailia. Behind the 2nd Division the 3rd Infantry Division was dug in across the central Ismailian road and the main road to Suez between Jebel Libni and Bir Hassana. In the south the 6th Infantry Division, based on Kuntilla and Nakhl, covered the Pilgrim's Way which ran from Kuntilla and Ras-el-Nagb near the Israeli border to Suez. All five infantry divisions had three infantry brigades, each of which was supported with a battalion of T-34 tanks or SU-100 self propelled guns and a battalion of Schmel anti-tank missiles. The 4th Division, equipped with the newest and best of the Soviet tanks, was held in reserve in the Bir Gifgaga area while the second and smaller of the two armoured divisions covered the Nakhl and Thamad areas on the routes into Sinai from Kuntilla and Ras-el-Nagb. (This division was not officially constituted as the 2nd Armoured Division, although it is often referred to as such. It was, in fact, known as Shazli Force after the name of its commander, and consisted of four tank battalions, a motorized infantry brigade, a commando battalion and three artillery regiments.)

This deployment presented a strong defence; it also provided an excellent springboard for offensive action. By thrusting eastwards across the southern Negev, Shazli Force and the 6th Infantry Division could join hands with Jordan and cut off Eilat. Israel would thus be deprived of her port on the Gulf of Akaba, the proposed British and American-backed Red Sea Regatta would have no future, and Nasser would have gained a valuable bargaining counter if and when the UN intervened to impose a ceasefire.

In the 1956 campaign the Israelis had begun their assault up the central route and along the roads into Sinai from Eilat and the frontier post of Kuntilla. They had been able to do so and to make a dash down the coast to Sharm El-Sheikh because the Egyptian forces in the north of Sinai were weak, owing to the greater part of the Egyptian Army being deployed on the west side of the Suez Canal to resist the Anglo-French invasion. Because the circumstances were very different the Israelis could not repeat the same strategy. But they could try to make the Egyptians believe that they would. And just as the Israeli Air Force succeeded in persuading the Egyptians to move aircraft from the north, which was to be the theatre of operations, to the vicinity of the Red Sea an Israeli army deception plan also succeeded. From aerial photographs taken by an Egyptian reconnaissance aircraft during the week before the outbreak of war the Egyptians concluded that an Israeli force of two or three armoured brigades had concentrated between Mizpe Ramon and Suiwila opposite Kuntilla. In fact there was only one brigade; the rest of the tanks and vehicles appearing on the photographs were carefully camouflaged dummies.

In the land battle, as in the air, the Israeli tactics were based on surprise and speed. They were the same tactics as General Dayan had employed in his 1956 campaign in the Sinai. 'The enemy will be given no time too reorganize after the assault, and there will be no pause in the fighting', he wrote in his reconstruction of that war, *Diary of the Sinai Campaign*. 'We shall organize separate forces for each of the main objectives, and it will be the task of each force to get these in one continuous battle, one long breath to fight and push on, fight and push on, until the objective is gained.'

Israel's main objectives in the Sinai were much the same as they had been in 1956: to break the back of the Egyptian army on its borders, then to sprint forward to seize the range of mountains just east of the Suez Canal, to cut off the Egyptian escape routes. Once the Egyptian army was defeated the opening of the Straits of Tiran would follow automatically. The Israelis were confident in their ability to defeat the Egyptians; their difficulties centred on the terrain. The few roads which do exist in Sinai are rough and separated from each other by rocky ridges or by shifting sand-seas. Movement from east to west is not easy, and laterally from north to south, it is barely possible at all. Yet the war would have to be fought and won in Sinai, for the Israelis could not afford to let their country become the battlefield. They would have to move forward to meet the enemy which, in effect, meant an invasion.

For this invasion the Israeli forces were grouped into three highly mobile *Ugdas* commanded by Brigadiers Tal, Yoffe and Sharon respectively. Brigadier Gavish, GOC of Israel's Southern Command, was in overall command of the operations in this area; as such his authority was analogous to that of a corps commander. The exercise of this authority was, however, largely restricted to broad directives to the separate *Ugda* commanders rather than the issue of precise orders. Tal's *Ugda* of two armoured brigades, to which was attached the regular paratroop brigade (less one battalion which fought with the Sharon *Ugda*) had the elite of the Israeli Armoured Corps – 300 tanks, 100 half-tracks and about 50 guns many of which were self-propelled. The Sharon *Ugda* consisted of one armoured brigade, an infantry brigade, a paratroop battalion and six regiments of artillery – totalling about 200 tanks, 100 half-tracks and about 100 guns. Yoffe, whose *Ugda* was composed entirely of reservists, had two armoured brigades and a battalion of mechanized infantry – 200 tanks, 100 half-tracks, but no guns. Like American or British divisions, each *Ugda* was completely self-contained, with its own engineers, signals and medical units; it also had its own supply vehicles carrying fuel, ammunition and rations for three days of war. Many of these vehicles were 'reserves' too: civilian laundry lorries, ice-cream trucks and similar vehicles which had been commandeered for the duration.

Gavish's three *Ugdas* constituted the striking force. Three other bri-

Israeli tanks in action near Rafah junction

gades deployed along the Sinai front were regarded as reserves which could be thrust into the fighting later. One infantry brigade faced the Gaza Strip, one armoured brigade was positioned opposite Kusseima, and the third brigade – also armoured – faced Kuntilla. The defence of Eilat was in the hands of a single infantry battalion.

Mention has already been made of the deception measures taken in an effort to persuade the Egyptians that the Israelis were planning a dash down the coast road to seize Sharm El-Sheikh and open the Straits of Tiran. The real plan envisaged a three-pronged thrust, directed towards the Gaza Strip, El Arish, and Kusseima. Tal was charged with the difficult task of breaking into the Gaza Strip. His troops would storm the defences of Rafah, the hinge between the Strip and Egypt proper, and then move down towards El Arish. Meanwhile Yoffe's troops would battle their way across the desert to block the flow of Egyptian reinforcements to the Gaza region, and ultimately join Tal's men in a combined assault on El Arish. Sharon's task was to seize Abu Ageila, where the junction of roads from El Arish, Jebel Libni and Kusseima effectively blocked the main line of advance of Israeli forces into Sinai's central region.

Tal decided to break into the Gaza Strip by way of Khan Yunis, a town east of Rafah. This meant crossing a formidable minefield, and tackling

part of the 20th Palestinian Division as well as troops of the Egyptian 7th Division – all of whom were well dug-in and supported by well-sited anti-tank guns. As the Egyptians had laid a continuous belt of mines along the entire border of the Strip there was little to commend any one particular crossing place over any other. Once his armour had smashed or cleared a passage through the minefield it could fan out and use the roads inside the Strip, as the latter were unlikely to have been mined. The chief advantage in Khan Yunis as the nodal point for the Israeli assault derived, however, from the fact that it would be almost out of range of the guns of the T-54 tanks which the Egyptians were using to cover the town of Gaza. (The Gaza Strip, occupied by more than 750,000 people – many of them Palestinian refugees – is poor tank country, and the Egyptians had dug pits for the T-54s.) Once Tal's tanks had penetrated the Egyptian defences they would turn west to attack Rafah; when Rafah was taken the armour would continue along the coast road to El Arish. Behind them the reserve brigade which had been deployed opposite the Strip would clear the area and round up the remaining Egyptians.

This was to be the first land battle of the war and it was deemed to be the most important. No matter what the cost, the Israelis had to win. 'If we are to win the war', Tal told his men, 'we must win the first battle. The battle must be fought with no retreats, every objective must be taken – no matter what the cost in casualties. We must succeed or die . . .' This 'regardless of cost' policy was pursued until it became obvious that the war was won. Counted in blood the bill was high: official Israeli casualties for the fighting in Sinai were given as 275 killed and 800 wounded, which – expressed in American Vietnam terms (taking into account America's hundredfold larger population) would be around 27,500 dead and 80,000 wounded. But the Israeli commanders knew that failure would have been disastrous and in the long run would have resulted in even more casualties. Israeli morale would have suffered, and Egyptian morale would have received a corresponding boost.

Shortly after 8am on the first morning of the war Tal received the green light for the Sinai offensive in the form of code-words Beni Or (Sons of Light, after the theme of the Dead Sea Scrolls), and Sadin Adom (Red Sheet). The first wave of Israeli planes was already on its way to the Egyptian airfields, and by the time Tal's tanks crossed the Sinai border half the Egyptian Air Force had been reduced to a charred mess of twisted metal. But neither the Israeli crews nor the Egyptian soldiers in Gaza knew anything of this.

As a battalion of Pattons, closely followed by another battalion of Centurions, raced across the desert towards the minefield, Israeli Fouga Magisters flew in to attack Egyptian artillery near Rafah. The assault was made on a front of just over half-a-mile wide and, as expected, mines accounted for the first Israeli casualties. Many of these mines were plastic, and as they could not be found with mine detectors, the Israelis made no attempt to clear them. The mines, other anti-tank obstacles, and surprisingly stiff Egyptian resistance slowed the Israelis' progress considerably. Casualties both in men and vehicles, were heavy – although some of the tanks were quickly repaired and were soon back in action. Because the Israeli tank commanders habitually advanced with open turrets and signalled manually from them, in action their casualty rate was high. The Israelis defended the practice on the grounds that the tank commanders had a better view and could react more quickly than their battened-down enemies. In a battle, where the cost is secondary to the achievement of the objective it may be justified, in other circumstances the loss of trained tank commanders may well hazard future operations.

Once his two battalions of tanks had crossed the minefield and broken through the outer crust of defences, Tal's original plan was for the leading battalion of Pattons to crash through Khan Yunis while the second battalion of Centurions veered west, bypassing the town and then down the main road to Rafah. Approaching Khan Yunis, however, the Pattons came under heavy fire from the Beni Souhila ridge to the east, and it was clear that the town was held in far greater strength than had been supposed. A quick change of plan followed. Bypassing the ridge, the Pattons attacked Khan Yunis from the north-west while the Centurions charged forward into the town instead of circling round it. As the converging columns of tanks pounded through the streets, white flags began to flutter from the shuttered windows and the firing died down. Pattons met Centurions in the market square where posters advertised the current film showing at the main cinema. By some ironic quirk of fate this was entitled 'Help'. Sniping was to break out again later when the tanks resumed their advance and remnants of the Palestinian garrison ventured out of their hiding places. But the Israelis had attained their first objective. Leaving a company of infantry to mop up the town the Pattons and Centurions moved westwards towards Rafah.

Here again the Israelis were surprised by the strength and resistance of the defenders. A brigade of the 7th Egyptian Infantry Division and a battalion of the Palestinians supported by about 150 Js-3 tanks and 90 guns were holding four localities north and south of the town, and when the Israeli tanks appeared heavy fire was brought down on them. Tank after tank went up in flames as groups of anti-tank guns fired ten round salvoes. 'We left there [at Rafah] many of our dead soldiers and burnt-out tanks' the Israeli brigade commander told a press conference later. To continue with the frontal attack would clearly be suicidal, so another bypass was ordered. Swinging round the Egyptian positions, the tanks headed west to crash through the main street of Sheikh Zuweid, surprise its Egyptian garrison, and destroy an unsuspecting convoy of Egyptian vehicles on its way to a supply centre nearby. From there Tal's armour clattered on to the mouth of the Jiradi Pass about ten miles beyond Sheikh Zuweid. Seven miles long, the narrow pass was held by one of the brigades of the 7th Egyptian Infantry Division, supported by T-34 tanks and artillery, and its approaches were heavily mined. The Egyptians were not expecting to be attacked. But without pausing, the Centurions roared straight into the pass and were almost through the defences before the defenders reacted. Only the last two of the Centurions were hit, but the Israeli convoy of lightly-armoured and thin-skinned supporting vehicles which was following was stopped by a devastating hail of fire. Meantime the Centurions had rattled on through the pass to the outskirts of El Arish unaware that they were on their own. There they stopped, to await the rest of the brigade which they assumed would be coming up behind them and for dusk when El Arish was scheduled to be hit by an Israeli air strike.

While all this was happening two battalions of Tal's attached parachute brigade had been driving across country further to the south. This force was heading for an old disused road running south from Rafah which the Israelis believed would provide an unopposed route into the Strip and enable them to get behind the Egyptian defences of Rafah. Good progress was made to the road and when it was reached the advance guard turned north – only to be stopped when the leading Patton tanks came under intense fire. A brigade of the 7th Egyp-

tian Infantry Division, supported by about 100 guns, 35 JS-35s and some T-34s, was deployed across this southern approach to Rafah, and from their well prepared defences the Egyptians were prepared to offer stout resistance. The Israeli Pattons charged the defensive perimeter head-on, and although their company commander – leaning out of the turret of his tank – was killed, the tanks crashed through the first line of Egyptian defence. But their troubles were only just beginning. At a second line of trenches the tanks were stopped by more anti-tank fire and the guns of some IS-3s. In the circumstances all they could do was to sheer away and these Pattons with a company of paratroops eventually carried on to the Rafah-El Arish road. There they had a successful little engagement in which they knocked out twenty-two Egyptian tanks. Meantime the main force of paratroops, following in half-tracks, had run straight into the trouble which had forced the Pattons off course. Halted and pinned down by fire, the commander quickly realized that he was not going to be able to fight his own way out of the situation, and he signalled Tal asking for help. Now that there was little danger of interference by Egyptian aircraft, the Israeli Air Force was able to cope with situations like this. Fouga Magisters quickly appeared on the scene to bomb and strafe the Egyptians in front of the paratroops. Tal also despatched a column of tanks to relieve the pressure, but the Egyptians had begun to pull out before they approached the battlefield. Battling their way forward against diminishing resistance, the paratroops cleared the area of pockets of defenders. Exhausted, scattered and urgently in need of fuel, the brigade reached the outskirts of Rafah as night descended.

Judging by the number of burnt out and disabled vehicles littering the Rafah-El Arish road by this time, the Egyptians had already suffered defeat. But the Gaza Strip behind Tal was still holding out. In Khan Yunis, which had been overrun in the morning, groups of Palestinians from the 20th Palestinian Division had formed pockets of resistance when the Israelis moved west. These groups had plenty of anti-tank weapons and the task of rooting them out eventually had to be undertaken by the paratroops who had fought the exhausting battle south of Rafah.

An Egyptian soldier surrenders from his dugout between Rafah and El Arish

The town of Gaza, capital of the Strip and the headquarters of the Egyptian administration, was even more fiercely defended. Both Gaza and Khan Yunis constituted a threat to further Israeli advances while they were unoccupied, and as Gaza had political significance it was decided to capture it first. At dawn on Tuesday, the Second Day, four battalions of infantry and a battalion of Sherman tanks began to close in on the town from several directions. Their advance was covered by a heavy bar-, rage of mortar and artillery fire, followed by a bombing strike by the Israeli Air Force, now jubilant at the victories of the day before. In this attack fourteen UNEF soldiers were killed and twenty-five wounded when the UN building in Gaza where they were awaiting repatriation was hit by mortar fire. In the streets a fierce battle developed as the tanks literally shot their way into the centre of the town; while this was going on the civilian population cowered in hastily dug shelters. By Tuesday night the Israelis had the centre of Gaza and General Abdul Monan Husseini the Military Governor formally surrendered the town at 10.20am on Wednesday morning. Sporadic fighting and sniping continued in Gaza for two more days while the Israelis combed out the Egyptians house by house. But as soon as it was clear that the back of the resistance was broken the Israelis turned their attention to Khan Yunis. Groups of Palestinians

Below: Gaza is captured, and Israel's tank units take up positions dominating the town's main square. *Above:* General Abdul Monan Husseini, commander of the Gaza garrison, is taken into captivity. *Above right:* Some of Gaza's male population, wearing civilian clothes, are moved off into captivity

resisted stubbornly and there was a good deal of hard fighting before they were winkled out. Many of their positions fought on until they were actually overrun by tanks and it was Wednesday night before the Israelis could claim that resistance had completely collapsed.

While Tal's forces had been battling round Rafah one brigade of Yoffe's *Ugda*, twenty miles further south, had advanced across a sea of sand dunes towards Bir Lahfan, where it would be in a good position to prevent Egyptian reinforcements being sent to El Arish. Believing that the camel track running from the frontier to Bir Lahfan was impassable to vehicles the Egyptians were content to scatter a few mines and leave it unblocked. Loose sand made the going slow and Yoffe's Centurions took nine hours to cover thirty miles. Apart from a skirmish with the garrison of an Egyptian outpost and a fleeting glimpse of some Egyptian vehicles, however, the tanks reached the Abu Ageila-Bir Lahfan

بوابة النصر

road without incident. But when the leading tanks turned up the road towards Bir Lahfan and El Arish they came under fire. In the fading daylight further progress was not now possible, so the Centurions turned off the road to take up positions from which they could ambush any vehicles approaching the Bir Lahfan road junction from the south. Soon after dark they were joined by the rest of the brigade. Barely had the brigade settled into position when a convoy of vehicles was seen approaching from the direction of Jebel Libni. As expected the Egyptians were trying to reinforce their troops in El Arish, and these vehicles constituted elements of an armoured brigade and part of a mechanized infantry brigade. The Israelis waited until the Egyptian convoy was almost on them; when they opened fire, their first shots hit three T-55 tanks. For a few moments the convoy was thrown into confusion, and all lights on the Egyptian vehicles were extinguished. Both sides started then to shoot at each other and fighting continued intermittently throughout the night.

Further south Ariel Sharon's *Ugda* had run into trouble. Sharon, it will be recalled, had been given the task of breaking into Sinai along the so-called Central Route. His objective was the Abu Ageila road junction, and before he could get there he had to smash through a strongly fortified position on the Um Katif plateau about fifteen miles west of the Israeli border. Because the roads from El Arish, Jebel Libni and Kusseima all met at Abu Ageila and the key to Abu Ageila was Um Katif, there was no alternative to a direct assault. The Israelis could not afford to advance further into Sinai while leaving such a strongly held position behind them. Nor could Yoffe's second brigade advance until Abu Ageila had been taken. Like Tal's break-in operation this assault was considered to be in the 'regardless of cost' category.

Young Israeli soldiers remove an Egyptian sign at Gaza, leaving their own flag to signify the new occupation

At Um Katif the Egyptians were firmly established in defences ideally suited to the tactics they and their Russian advisers preferred. Their main position centred on a long low ridge, wedged between a sand-sea to the north and a rocky mountain massif known as Jebel Dalfa on the south. Behind a protective minefield 300 yards deep, three parallel lines of trenches nearly three miles long had been dug – with 300 yards between first and second – and 600 yards between the second and third lines. Concrete emplacements had been set at intervals along the trenches, and each line was held by an infantry battalion of the Egyptian 2nd Infantry Division. To support them, about ninety T-34s and SU-100s had been deployed and dug in behind the forward perimeter; further back, six regiments of artillery equipped with 122mm guns promised further support, and Schmel anti-tank projectors had been liberally distributed among the lines of infantry.

Sharon's original plan of attack was based on the premise that the Um Katif position was held by only one Egyptian battalion – which was in fact true until two days before the war started. As the cost in men and material was secondary to success, he decided that a direct frontal assault offered the best chance of a speedy break-through. Thus, shortly before 9am on the Monday morning Fouga Magisters struck the Egyptian positions and Sharon's Centurion battalion – followed by a company of mechanized infantry – charged across the undulating ground which lay between the Sinai border and the Um Katif. At the minefield, where seven of the Centurions were disabled, the charge came to a halt, and Sharon saw that he was not going to break into Um Katif by way of the front door. Another air strike was called up, and in this attack one of the

El Arish airbase is taken from the Egyptians, and the Israeli flag is secured to the masthead

planes was shot down – a fact which no doubt provided tremendous encouragement to the Egyptians. Meantime Sharon had ordered the Centurions which had survived the minefield to veer northwards round the Um Katif plateau and follow a camel track which eventually joined the Abu Ageila road. At the same time his battalion of Shermans which had been advancing behind the Centurions were told to take over the front attack and to crash through Um Katif. During the air strike the Shermans were able to make some progress but as soon as the planes turned away the Egyptian guns poured a concentrated volume of fire on the advancing tanks, which compelled them to stop.

The Centurions, struggling up the camel track in single file, had also been brought to a halt and compelled to shelter among the sand dunes. From their positions both the Centurions and the Shermans were able to shoot into the Egyptian defences. But they were pinned down by Egyptian fire even after dark, and any attempt to make another frontal assault would clearly have been suicidal. Sharon decided that his best means of breaking the impasse lay in an infantry assault on the flank of the Egyptian position. So his infantry brigade was put into civilian buses and motored as far forward as the two-wheeled drive vehicles could get before they were bogged down in the sand. This was not far, and the heavily-laden infantry had to march the rest of the way. With ten miles still to go it was several hours before they reached the area from which they would be ready to assault and 'roll up' the lines of Egyptian trenches.

While his infantry were tramping through the sand Sharon had been considering how best to silence the Egyptian artillery, and he had decided to give this task to his independent paratroop battalion. Having been promised twelve helicopters to lift the battalion into action he planned to put the paratroops down in the desert about three miles north of the Egyptian gun position. They would then attack at the same time as the main assault went in on Um Katif. In the event only six helicopters arrived, and when they were spotted landing in the desert the Egyptians mortared the landing zone and forced them to move back. This meant that the paratroops had farther to march, and the time of the combined assault to be put back. When Sharon received a signal saying that the air strikes he had asked for to soften up Um Katif had had to be called off (Jordan had entered the war and the Israeli Air Force's resources were being diverted to the fighting for Jerusalem), it seemed as if his *Ugda* was dogged by misfortune. But Sharon refused to be daunted. Massing his artillery, the biggest concentration of fire ever shot by the Israelis was put down on the Egyptian trench system. It was nearly midnight when this barrage was lifted, and the Israeli infantry, carrying coloured lights to show their positions to their gunner observers behind, launched their attack.

As the Israelis moved systematically along the parapets of the Egyptian trenches, shooting down into the firing bays, the Egyptians scrambled to the shelter of their dugouts. Two miles west of this battle, the paratroops has also gone into action. They had reached the Egyptian artillery without undue difficulty, although the going through deep soft sand was a fatiguing business, and in one rush they had overrun some of the gun positions. But the Egyptians had rallied and the Israeli paratroops found themselves pinned down by small arms fire. When dawn came up at 4am they had four dead and thirteen wounded; and as the Israelis never abandoned their casualties the need for two men to carry each body reduced the effective strength of the original 150-strong paratroop force by a third. By this time, however, the battle for the trenches had reached a stage which enabled Sharon to call off the paratroop operation. With a mile of trenches already cleared, the armour was able to resume its advance on Sharon's real objective, Abu Ageila. So, as the Shermans ground forward up and over Um Katif and then westwards along the axis of the road to Abu Ageila, the paratroops were ordered to pull out, and make their way through the sand dunes to the road east of Um Katif. At 6am the battle was by no means over, but the road through Abu Ageila to Jebel Libni and beyond was open. Sharon's infantry brigade spent the rest of the day winkling out the Egyptians who still remained at Um Katif, while Sharon himself collected his armoured brigade and took it off to deal with Kusseima.

Yoffe's second armoured brigade (two battalions of Centurions and a mechanized infantry battalion) had been impatiently waiting for Sharon's troops to open the road through Abu Ageila. As soon as the Shermans fought their way past Um Katif, Yoffe's Centurions trundled up to the Abu Ageila road junction. There they turned north, heading towards Bir Lahfan where Centurions of Yoffe's other brigade, with their backs to the Egyptian defences at Bir Lahfan, were having a tough battle with two Egyptian armoured brigades. To enable them to get through to Abu Ageila hundreds of Sharon's support vehicles – buses, milk trucks and almost every other form of civilian transport which had been pressed into service – had to be pushed clear of the track into the sand.

Once past the road junction the Israeli Centurions roared up to the Bir Lahfan tank battle, coming up behind on the flanks of the Egyptian T-55s. For some time the Egyptians fought back but they had been pounded by the Israeli Air Force since first light, and the Israeli Centurions, whose hitting power was greater than that of the T-55s, turned the scales. By 10am the Egyptians had had enough, the survivors broke off the action to turn westward into the desert. Behind them they left the victorious Israeli Centurions to re-assemble amid the broken and smouldering wreckage of many Egyptian vehicles.

With the Egyptian armour now in full retreat, Jebel Libni, where the Egyptians had built a large airfield, became the next objective of the Israelis in their advance into Central Sinai. Thus, as soon as his tanks were refuelled, Yoffe set off with one of his armoured brigades south-west towards Jebel Libni. Following close behind came Tal with one of his armoured brigades; some distance behind that the second of Tal's armoured brigades. Back at the Abu Ageila road junction the column turned west along the Central Route, and the leading tanks reached the outskirts of Jebel Libni about 4pm. As Yoffe's tanks swung left, Tal's leading brigade swung right to complete a pincer move which snapped tight on the airfield. As the Israeli tanks charged towards each other from opposite sides of the airfield, Israeli planes dived on Egyptian tanks deployed on and around the airfield. Several of these tanks were destroyed and others left their positions to rumble off westwards into the desert. Seeing their tanks were leaving Egyptian infantrymen and gunners also left their positions and ran off into the desert. But the airfield was still strongly defended and the two Israeli brigades spent the night (Tuesday/Wednesday) on opposite sides of the airfield, resting, refuelling and planning a dawn attack.

At daybreak all went as the Israelis had planned; the Egyptian opposition suddenly collapsed and the airfield was quickly captured. Yoffe and Tal now parted company, with Yoffe's brigade taking the road south to Bir Hassana while Tal's force headed towards Bir Gifgata to block the Central Route through the hills leading to Ismailia. Yoffe's advance guard arrived at Bir Hassana about 9am on the morning of the third day (Wednesday). Racing towards their objective the Israeli tanks had over-taken and often intermingled with columns of retreating Egyptian vehicles. In their haste to get away some of the Egyptian tanks fired at each other as well as at the Israelis; others simply left the road and drove off into the desert. In the event there was little opposition at Bir Hassana, which was lucky for the Israelis because Yoffe's prime concern now was to get ahead to the Mitla and Giddi Passes. Here he would be able to block the Egyptian escape routes and so cut off both the 'Shazli' Armoured Division and the 6th Egyptian Infantry Division whose troops were deployed along the 'Pilgrims' Way' between El Thamed and Nakhel.

Yoffe's Centurions were now beginning to show signs of the hammering to which they had been subjected over the past three days, and when it came to leaving Bir Hassana only twenty 'runners' could be mustered. And by the time he reached the eastern end of the Mitla Pass only nine of these were running under their own power, and they were perilously short of fuel. The remainder had either run out of petrol or were suffering from mechanical defects. As the column approached the mouth of the pass other columns of retreating Egyptians coming across the desert converged on them. But as the Egyptians also had Centurions the Israeli tanks were assumed to be theirs and without interference they were allowed to take up positions near the Parker Memorial, the stone monument to a former British administrator set on a hummock near the mouth of the pass. Once in position, the Israeli tanks were not long in showing which side they were on. Egyptian vehicles approaching the pass were either destroyed, damaged or dispersed; and the mouth of the pass soon became a graveyard cluttered with wrecked trucks and tanks. In the fading light a few vehicles did manage to weave their way through this litter, but they were bombed and strafed by the Israeli Air Force as they moved through the pass.

Further north a similar scenario was being enacted at the Ismailia Pass, a few miles west of Bir Gifgafa. But here the Israelis did not fare so well. After leaving Jebel Libni, Tal's force had run into trouble at Bir Hamma, where a brigade of the 3rd Egyptian Infantry Division supported by a battalion of T-34s and some SU-100 guns was defending the airfield. Under the cover of an Israeli air strike Tal's Centurions charged the Egyptian positions. Within half an hour the battle was over, and the Egyptians had fled into the desert. With his reserve brigade now taking the lead, Tal's force sped westward again along the road to Bir Gifgafa. En route there was a brief exchange of fire between Tal's Pattons and some Egyptian T-55s, and when the Egyptians broke off and fled their supply vehicles fell into Israeli hands. For Tal, whose vehicles – like those of Yoffe – were now running desperately short of petrol, this was welcome booty indeed.

Bir Gifgafa was surrounded by a sprawling complex of military installations. But it was the fact that the lateral road from Bir Thamada terminated here which was the important issue for Tal at this time. Yoffe had been ordered to block the Mitla and Giddi Passes in the south, and if the retreating Egyptians could not get past him only the Ismailia Pass remained open to them. As the Israeli tanks left Bir Gifgafa to attack the defensive positions at the mouth of the pass there was a clear indication that the Egyptians were already being forced to use this escape route. A cloud of dust disclosed the approach of a long column of vehicles; it was part of the Egyptian 4th Armoured Division which had been ordered to fall back to take up positions on the Central Ridge behind the Ismailia Pass. Tal promptly ordered every tank he had in the area to attack the Egyptians in the flank. So began a bloody battle which continued until night descended – by which time the Israelis had exhausted most of the ammunition and fuel. About a dozen T-55 tanks and 50 Egyptian armoured personnel carriers were destroyed and hundreds of Egyptian soldiers were killed in the course of the fighting. The Israelis also suffered heavy casualties, however, and – for the first time since the beginning of the war – Egyptian planes appeared over the battlefield. Israeli aircraft were quickly on the scene, but in the ensuing dogfights one Israeli plane returning from a raid in the Canal area was shot down.

Although Tal's forces had inflicted heavy punishment, the fact remains that it had failed to close the vital Ismailia Pass. All that night vehicles of the 4th Egyptian Armoured Division streamed through it, and the Israelis had to stand up to a strong counterattack which drove them back from the positions they had taken up to harass the traffic approaching the pass. But when dawn broke on the morning of the Fourth Day, Thursday, Tal's tanks returned to the battle – reinforced, reorganized and refuelled. When they began their advance, slowly and methodically clearing the series of defensive positions which obstructed them, the Egyptians steadily gave ground. Yet again the Centurions demonstrated their superiority over the T-54s and T-55s which the Egyptians had deployed along the five-mile stretch of road leading to the mouth of the pass. The Israeli planes, which signalled the exact location of the Egyptian tanks and then dropped napalm on them, can also be credited with making a major contribution to the success of the operation. By 4pm some forty Egyptian tanks had been destroyed for the loss of only two Israeli tanks, and shortly after that the Egyptians broke off the battle, withdrew their tanks and tried to get them back through the pass. Crammed with vehicles frantically trying to force their way back towards the Canal, the Ismailia road became a bombers' dream, which the Israeli Air Force was not slow to take advantage of. Blazing napalm and bombs created an inferno from which the only escape was on foot.

Behind the fleeing Egyptians the Israeli Centurions crashed through the pass, dragging or pushing wrecked and disabled vehicles aside to clear the way for Tal's Patton battalion to race through to the Suez Canal. The Egyptians had had neither time nor opportunity to organize any defensive line between the Ismailia Pass and there was virtually no opposition between there and the Canal crossings. Everything had happened so quickly and the confusion, consequent on the false information fed to them by the Arab radio had been so complete, many Egyptians could not comprehend the extent of the military disaster which had overtaken them. When Tal's leading Pattons approached the Canal in the early hours of the morning of Friday 9th June Egyptians on the Canal bank flagged them down with flashing torches, thinking that the Pattons were Egyptian tanks making for the bridge across the Canal.

Tanks from Yoffe's *Ugda* reached the Canal bank farther south about two hours after Tal arrived opposite Ismailia. Setting out from the eastern end of the Mitla Pass at dawn on the Thursday (the fourth day) it was noon before Yoffe's vehicles emerged at the Egyptian end, fifteen miles away. As at the Ismailia Pass the narrow road through Mitla was choked with the debris of war, and many burnt-out and wrecked vehicles had to be pushed aside before the Israeli tanks could get through. When they did arrive at the western end of the pass they were met by Israeli paratroops who had been put down by helicopter to seal off the pass. Meantime Yoffe's other armoured brigade had raced twenty miles north from Mitla to block the sole remaining avenue of Egyptian escape:the Giddi Pass. Under cover of darkness many Egyptian vehicles had already slipped through this pass and a battalion of T-55s and T-54s remained in its defence when the Israelis arrived on the scene. The same tactics as Tal had employed at the Ismailia Pass were repeated here, and by 7pm Yoffe's tanks and Israeli aircraft had shot, bombed, strafed and napalmed a clear route through the Pass. From its western mouth the Canal was less than 30 miles distant and Centurions raced forward to take up positions opposite Port Suez.

Troops of a composite Israeli force which had motored along the coast road from El Arish were, in fact, the first to reach the Canal. Starting out in the early hours of Wednesday morning, after mopping up operations in Khan Yunis were considered as good as over, a scratch force had charged along the road with headlights blazing. Israeli aircraft had reported that the Egyptians appeared to have no set defences between El Arish and the Canal, so it was possible to throw caution to the winds. Apart from a few shots fired by the bewildered occupants of supply dumps and staging camps as the Israeli vehicles roared past, there was, in fact, no opposition until the Israelis passed Romani, a small coastal town about forty miles from Port Said. Shortage of fuel compelled a halt here, and the Israelis snatched a few hours rest before setting off again at dawn on Thursday morning. By now the Egyptians had been alerted to their presence and the Israelis' progress was slowed by increasing opposition. Blocks held by Egyptian commando troops supported by T-55s brought delays; so too did a number of attacks by the Egyptian Air Force. A fierce

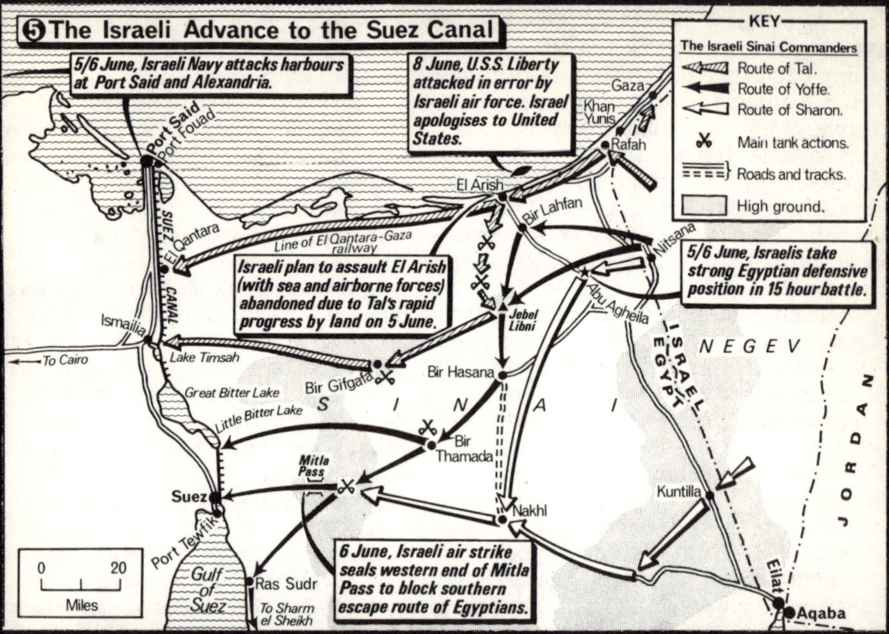

5 The Israeli Advance to the Suez Canal
5/6 June, Israeli Navy attacks harbours at Port Said and Alexandria.
8 June, U.S.S. Liberty attacked in error by Israeli air force. Israel apologises to United States.
KEY
The Israeli Sinai Commanders
Route of Tal.
Route of Yoffe.
Route of Sharon.
Main tank actions.
Roads and tracks.
High ground.
Gaza
Khan Yunis
Rafah
Port Said
Port Fouad
El Arish
Bir Lahfan
Nitsana
SUEZ CANAL
El Qantara
Line of El Qantara-Gaza railway
Israeli plan to assault El Arish (with sea and airborne forces) abandoned due to Tal's rapid progress by land on 5 June.
5/6 June, Israelis take strong Egyptian defensive position in 15 hour battle.
Jebel Libni
Abu Agheila
Ismailia
To Cairo
Lake Timsah
Bir Gifgafa
Bir Hasana
NEGEV
ISRAEL
EGYPT
JORDAN
Great Bitter Lake
Little Bitter Lake
SINAI
Bir Thamada
Mitla Pass
Suez
Kuntilla
Nakhl
Port Tewfik
6 June, Israeli air strike seals western end of Mitla Pass to block southern escape route of Egyptians.
0
20
Miles
Gulf of Suez
Ras Sudr
To Sharm el Sheikh
Eilat
Aqaba

battle developed a few miles from Kantara, a fair-sized town on the Canal bank – close to the El Firdan railway bridge, which the Egyptians were intent on holding to get some of their own tanks back across the Canal. When the Israeli Air Force was called in, however, the way was opened. At 8pm the first Israeli troops entered the now deserted town of Kantara and began to close in on the bridge. By dawn they had cleared the area of Egyptians, and had seized the Sinai end of the bridge. Soon after that a patrol from Tal's force opposite Ismailia contacted them on the Canal bank.

This virtually spelt the end of war in the Sinai. But the account would not be complete without an account of the vicissitudes of Sharon's *Ugda* after the battle at Um Katif, and of the seizure of Sharm El-Sheikh.

Sharon, with one armoured brigade had set off from Um Katif about 8am on the Wednesday morning (the third day.); his men, dog tired after the battle, had rested, and his vehicles had been replenished. Sharon's task now was to seek out and destroy the Shazli Armoured Division; but he was ordered to hold off until Kusseima had been secured by the independent armoured brigade which had been sitting opposite Kusseima and which so far had seen no action. As the 2nd Egyptian Infantry Division had been deployed in and around Kusseima this was the logical course to take. In the event, however, the 2nd Egyptian Infantry had crept away while Sharon's men were sleeping and when the Israeli tanks probed cautiously forward the Egyptian positions were found to be deserted.

With Kusseima empty, Sharon's *Ugda* drove south towards Nakhl. Not until they were about twenty miles from Nakhl was there any opposition. Then, near a long ridge known as Jebel Karim, the leading vehicles ran into a minefield and a jeep was blown up. When the bullets began to fly, it seemed that the Israelis had arrived at the outposts of the 6th Egyptian Infantry Division and that Egyptians were still occupying their defences. As it was now dark, Sharon decided to halt, to refuel, to rest and to wait for daylight before trying to push on.

Once again his enemies slipped through Sharon's fingers. The main body of the Shazli Division, which Sharon had set out to destroy, was already haring back towards the Giddi Pass and the Egyptian rearguard slipped away while the Israelis sat the night out at the edge of the minefield. Nearly all the infantrymen from the brigade which had been holding the position where Sharon had called a half had also piled into their trucks and headed towards the Suez Canal, (although few of them got away because they ran into Yoffe's Centurions at the Mitla Pass, or were bombed out of existence by Israeli aircraft). Consequently when dawn broke on Thursday morning Sharon's troops faced an empty position; the only evidence of the Egyptians were abandoned tanks and guns.

So Sharon resumed his advance towards Nakhl, where he hoped to intercept the second brigade of the 6th Division. The latter had been deployed around Kuntilla but it had pulled out during the night, and set off back for Suez along the Pilgrims' Way. Sharon arrived at Nakhl before the Egyptians, blocked the Pilgrims' Way east of the town with a battalion of Shermans, and lined the eastern approach with concealed Centurions and mechanized infantry. The Egyptians drove straight into the ambush and were caught in criss-cross fire on the ground. Behind them followed the Israeli independent brigade which had faced them across the border opposite Kuntilla, so there was no going back. From above the relays of Israeli aircraft, which had pursued them from the moment they abandoned their defences, bombed, napalmed and strafed them. In desperation the Egyptians tried to fight their way past Sharon, but time and

Burned out vehicles and tanks line the road to Suez

Israeli troops set up a tank position in newly conquered territory close to the Suez canal

again they were beaten back. When night came and the fighting died down, the road between Thamed and Nakhl had taken on the now familiar appearance of the major defiles in Sinai, and was choked with destroyed and abandoned guns and vehicles.

So the Egyptian Army in Sinai was defeated. Sharm El-Sheikh was captured by a combined naval and paratroop operation and the Israeli flag was raised there on the Wednesday morning, (the third day). As military operations go, this one was of little significance since the Egyptians had withdrawn all but one company of infantry before the Israelis arrived. When the UN soldiers evacuated Sharm El-Sheikh on 23rd May they had destroyed the desalination plant and the Egyptian garrison sent in to take over was faced with the problem of getting fresh water. The few wells which existed were inadequate for the numbers of troops sent to Sharm El-Sheikh and water had to be shipped in from Suez. Until hostilities broke out this was feasible, but when war began the Israeli Air Force and three Israeli Motor Torpedo Boats operating from Eilat stopped water boats.

Following the occupation of Sharm El-Sheikh, sailors from the Israeli MTBs landed on Nas Nazrani and found it to be deserted. The Straits of Tiran, whose closure had precipitated the war, were now open to Israeli shipping and Eilat could breathe again. Finally, on Wednesday afternoon, a detachment of paratroops was flown in helicopters from Sharm El-Sheikh and set down at El Tur, a small oil centre in the Gulf of Suez, on the west coast of Sinai and about fifty miles from its tip. From there the paratroops moved north to link up with the Israelis on the Canal.

On Thursday 4th June Israel's flag flew all along the Suez Canal, and the Straits of Tiran were open. After only four days fighting the Egyptian air and land forces had been crushed: the sands of Sinai were strewn with the burnt-out wrecks of hundreds of armoured vehicles; about 300 tanks, 500 pieces of artillery, 10,000 trucks and vast quantities of other equipment had fallen into Israeli hands. Much of this equipment of Soviet origin, such as the TU-55 tanks and SU-57 self-propelled guns, was of considerable interest to the NATO countries – as was the equipment and layout of the SAM missile site which was overrun between the Mitla Pass and the Canal.

Egyptian casualties ran into thousands: how many thousands is

One of the casualties of the advance to Suez: a soldier receives attention in the field

still a matter for speculation. Egyptian figures published at the end of June 1967 stated that 5,000 soldiers had been killed in action. Some months later Nasser said that some 1,500 officers and 10,000 soldiers had been killed and that 500 officers and 5,000 soldiers had been taken prisoner. On these figures the number of wounded could run as high as 50,000 or even more. Prisoners, to the Israelis, were an embarrassment and they shuttled most of the hordes of men who succeeded in tramping across the desert across the Canal. Only the officers were held in captivity, and at the end of the war the Israelis announced that they had some 3,000.

Israeli casualties in Sinai were given as 275 killed and 800 wounded. The greater proportion of these were probably incurred in the 'break-in'

battles on the first and second days of the war when the Israelis' concern for success in battle outweighted consideration of the cost in terms of lives. On these two days also many Egyptians stood their ground and fought extremely well. Subsequently, when the Israeli Air Force had completed its prime task of destroying the Arab air forces and turned to the ground support of Israeli troops, the Egyptians' morale suffered and they did not fight so hard. The fact remains that the totality of the Egyptian defeat, and the brilliance of both conception and execution of the plan which brought Israel victory, almost defy belief.

Egyptian prisoners sit out the war in an improvised barbed-wire compound after the fall of Sharm El-Sheikh

Wreckage from the Egyptian army's war effort litters the Sinai desert

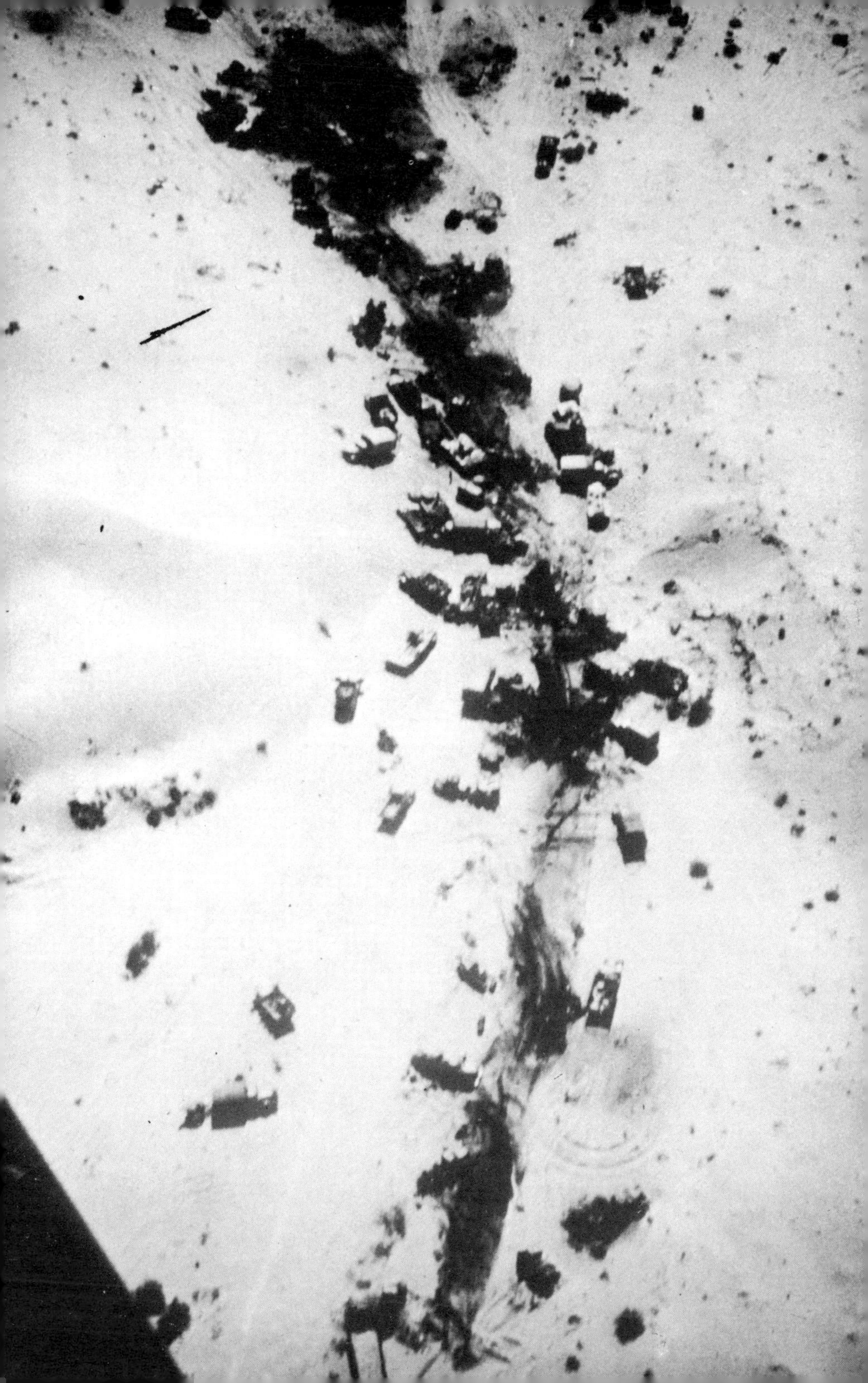

Israel displays some of the massive quantities of artillery captured intact during the desert fighting

The Central Front

Right up to the time the first Jordanian shells crashed down on the suburbs of New Jerusalem the Israelis had been hoping that Jordan would stay out of the war. It was a rational hope, but in the Middle East the rational things are the ones that are least likely to happen.

What was to be the final appeal for peace was made shortly after the outbreak of war with Egypt. In a message addressed to King Hussein which was sent via General Odd Bull, the UN Commander at Government House in Jerusalem, the Israeli Government promised that if Jordan would keep the peace, so too would they. This was a political promise to which Israel's military commanders gave their full support, for they had no desire to open a second front at this stage of the war. Faced by Jordan's seven infantry and two armoured brigades – five of which were deployed on the west bank of the Jordan – Israel's military resources could stretch only to the most modest provision for a holding action until the battle for Sinai had been resolved. And there was good reason to suppose that Hussein would hesitate before entering the war. Despite his recent pact with Nasser, the experience of 1956, Nasser's constant hostility right up to the signing of the pact and the fragility of the Jordanian Army, all provided grounds for believing that Hussein would opt for caution.

Unfortunately the emotional build-up in Jordan had swept pragmatic considerations aside and the optimistic Israeli conjectures were shattered at about 11am on 5th June. Until then Jerusalem was relatively quiet, and life went on much as usual. There were few signs of Israeli soldiers or military vehicles on the streets of New Jerusalem and the supermarket at the corner of the Avenue George V and Goshon Agron Street was so crowded and noisy that nobody heard the first shells. From the Arab heights above Jerusalem Jordanian artillery and mortars rained down on targets in the Israeli sector of the city, while long-range guns reached across Israel's narrow waist to hit the outskirts of Tel Aviv. Syrian artillery on the hills overlooking the Sea of Galilee was also firing on towns in northern Israel. But it was New Jerusalem which suffered the worst damage and most of its residents spent the next two days sheltering from the constant bombardment. Only those who were compelled to do so ventured above ground; yet more than 500 civilians were killed and wounded by Jordanian shells. None of the Jewish areas of the partitioned city were spared, and the houses of the Prime Minister, the Israeli President, and the Mayor of Jerusalem were all damaged by Jordanian shells. When the glass panels of showcases in the Israel Museum were shattered the Isaiah Scroll – the most complete of the Dead Sea Scrolls – was hastily moved to an underground vault. One of the famous Chagall stained-glass windows in the Hadassah Medical Centre's Synagogue was smashed, but the remainder were removed to safety before the tempo of the shelling increased. From France Chagall wrote: 'I am not worried about the windows, only about the safety of Israel. Let Israel be safe and I will make you lovelier windows.'

The Israelis did not return the

A member of an Israeli tank crew keeps watch on the Israeli-Jordan frontier

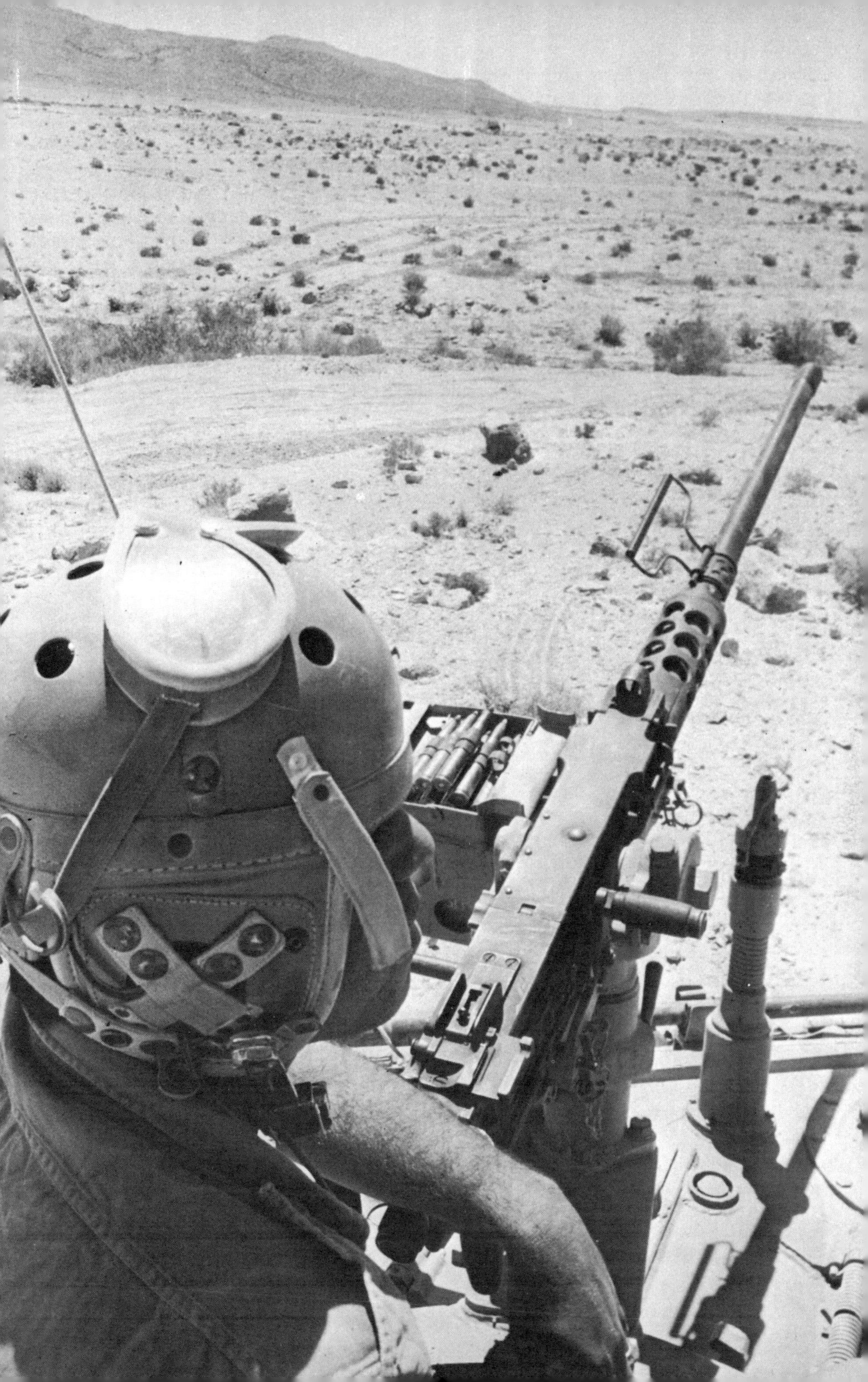

Jordanian fire for two hours. But as the shelling, mortar and small arms fire steadily got worse it was clear that an ugly situation was developing. Up to about noon on the Monday morning the Israelis clung to the belief that Hussein was merely trying to show Nasser that he was fulfilling his side of the military pact, and that he had no intention of putting up a serious fight. If he was determined to throw Jordan into the fight, however, Israel would not remain on the defensive. Israeli army intelligence had a shrewd idea of the Arab plan for 'recovering' Palestine and Jordan's role included a thrust west to link up with an Egyptian drive east across the Negev. If these attacks were to succeed Israel would be cut into three; and while the Negev attack might be contained, the geography of Israel gave a Jordanian thrust a passable chance of victory From the Jordan border it was only twelve miles to the Israeli coast at Tel Aviv – a determined armoured column could smash across that in a few hours. Israeli plans were therefore based on prevent-

ing the Jordanian's armour from rolling down to Tel Aviv, although the key to the opening stages of the battle was a political one – the Old City of Jerusalem. For a people to whom Jerusalem had such spiritual concern, this was the most precious goal. Without Jerusalem as its capital Israel could be compared to a body without its soul. But there were also good strategic reasons why the partition arrangement of 1948 should be amended. With Jerusalem and a wide access to the sea the Israelis would be able to consolidate their foothold in the Judean heartland, and there would no longer be the danger of their state degenerating into a coastal enclave clinging to the Mediterranean.

In essence, the Israeli plan was to isolate the battle for Jerusalem, while concentrating their main effort on the destruction of the Arab Legion formations along the entire length of the west bank of the Jordan. The plan was put into effect when the Israelis realized that Hussein was not going to be satisfied with a token gesture of support for the Arab cause.

It was an attempt to occupy Government House that triggered off the battle for Jerusalem. If only because Government House was in demilitarized territory and about 100 UN personnel were sheltering there, this was asking for trouble as it brought King Hussein into direct conflict with the United Nations. General Odd Bull, the UN commander, called for a cease fire but the Jordanians ignored the appeal, and by 1pm they had occupied the tiny wood which separated Government House from the adjacent farm. At this point the Israelis reacted.

Command of the Israeli troops in Jerusalem had been entrusted to Brigadier Uzi Narkiss, a veteran of what the Israelis would call their War of Independence. In 1948 he had fought as a battalion commander under Brigadier Yitzhak Rabin to hold Jerusalem, and it had been his sad duty to order a company under the command of Mordecai Gur to fall back from the Zion Gate. Rabin was now Chief of Staff, and Gur a brigade commander who was shortly to find himself again under Narkiss's command. All three – Rabin, Narkiss and Gur – were men born in Jerusalem who never hoped to see the Wailing Wall again. And now they might.

At 2.30pm on Monday afternoon, two companies of Israeli infantry and six Shermans crossed the 1948 armistice line and advanced on Government

Old Jerusalem

6 Israeli Advances in the Jerusalem Area

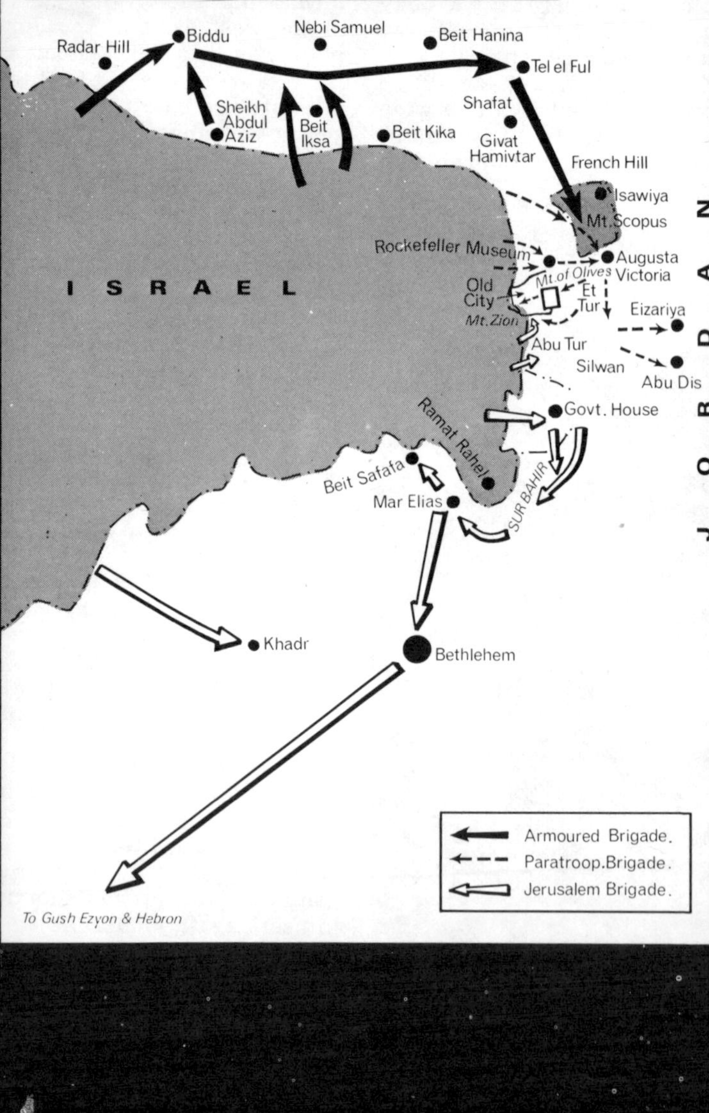

House. These troops were from one of the three battalions of the only Israeli brigade which Narkiss could call on at that time. Like the rest of the brigade the men were all reservists who lived and worked in the Jerusalem area – a fact which was to confer an immense advantage in the street fighting which was to come. By 3pm, following a brief and bloody encounter which cost the Israelis eight and the Jordanians eighteen dead, the Israeli flag was flying above Government House. This enabled General Odd Bull and the remainder of the UN personnel to be evacuated to Tel Aviv.

Meanwhile Jordanian forces in Samaria – the area which constituted the northern province of Jordan on the West Bank – had been reported by Israeli aircraft to be moving south. What the reconnaissance aircraft had seen was the 60th Jordanian Armoured Brigade trundling from Jericho towards Jerusalem, and its replacement the 40th Jordanian Armoured Brigade on its way from Damiya Bridge to Jericho. General Riad, the Egyptian general who was now directing Jordan's war against Israel, had persuaded Hussein to ask Syria for troops to block any Israeli sallies into northern Jordan and the West Bank. Confident that these reinforcements would soon be on their way he had ordered the 60th Brigade to move to the Ramallah Ridge, the sausage-shaped plateau which dominated the northern approach to Jerusalem and part of the Jewish quarters of the city. Realizing that if the Jordanians succeeded in establishing themselves on the ridge they would be able either to hit the Israeli forces in Jerusalem in the flank or to encircle them, Narkiss resolved to seize the ridge first. Now that battle was joined and the situation in Jerusalem promised a hard and tough fight Narkiss had been allocated more troops. The three battalions of a reservist armoured brigade which had assembled at Ramle was already

General Odd Bull

on its way towards Jerusalem; and a parachute brigade, consisting of one regular and two reserve battalions of paratroopers, which had been briefed for an airborne attack on El Arish was hurriedly diverted to Jerusalem. The paratroopers had no armoured vehicles, but they were tough and self-sufficient infantrymen ideally suited to tasks which Narkiss had in mind for them. Two other infantry brigades – one of which had concentrated near Latrun on Israel's geographical waist, and the other near Kalkiya – were also placed under Narkiss's command about the same time.

As soon as the armoured brigade arrived from Ramle, Narkiss threw it straight into the fray. Its objective was the Ramallah ridge, on which a three-pronged attack was mounted. As the approaches to the main ridge were heavily mined and the brigade had no flail tanks, Israeli infantrymen had to walk in front – probing and clearing a path for the Shermans which followed. Only six tanks were put out of action in the course of this advance, but it cost the lives or limbs of forty Israelis. Beyond the minefields the Jordanians were established in a number of concreted strongpoints: Radar Hill, Abdul Aziz Hill and the village of Beit Iksa. Each was tackled in succession, with the Shermans firing at point blank range into individual strongpoints until all Jordanian resistance ceased. By midnight the three Israeli columns had converged on the first crest of the main Ramallah Ridge. After clearing Biddu, a fortified village on the main ridge, the whole brigade turned east and moved along the road to Nebi Samuel – the burial place of the Prophet Samuel, which Christian Pilgrims throughout the ages have called the Hill of Joy. Aided by flares the Israeli tanks enveloped Nebi Samuel in a pincer movement, overran the key village of Beit Hanina and then swept on eastwards.

South of this road junction a battalion of Jordanian infantry was holding positions on the road leading to Jerusalem. As these positions blocked the way south to the Israeli enclave at Mount Scopus north-east of the Holy City, one of the Israeli armoured battalions was ordered to break through. However, just as the Israeli Shermans were getting into position to assault the outlying Jordanian position at Shafat, a battalion of Jordanian Pattons was seen to be heading towards Tel El Ful. It was one of the battalions of the 30th Armoured Brigade, en route from Jericho, which had been detailed to secure Tel El Ful. Swinging round, the Shermans just had time to gain the Ramallah road and get into ambush positions before the Pattons arrived. A bloody tank battle then ensued, with both sides slogging hard at each other at close range. When the Jordanians broke off at about 10am, six Pattons had been destroyed and eleven others were abandoned on the battlefield. Israeli casualties included three Shermans.

With Tel El Ful indisputably in their possession the Israelis now turned their attention back to Shafat. Following a combined armour and infantry attack Shafat quickly fell. The positions covering the defile of Givat Hamivtar were the next objective. These, and the defences of French Hill, completed the Jordanian defensive arc shielding Jerusalem from the north, and they were vital to the Jordanians. Tough resistance was met at Givat Hamivtar which had to be assaulted three times before the Jordanian defenders were overwhelmed. Even tougher resistance was met at French Hill, where five Israeli tanks were knocked out by Jordanian anti-tank weapons, and both sides sustained many casualties in bitter hand to hand fighting. By 5pm however, the Israelis had smashed their way through to their enclave on Mount Scopus, and the battle for Jerusalem was approaching its military climax.

In other sectors of the central front the Israelis were bent on smashing the Jordanians along the entire length of the west bank. While his armoured brigade was forcing its way up to the Ramallah Ridge in the north, Narkiss decided to cut the Jordanian road south from Jerusalem to Bethlehem. The battalion which had taken Government House was ordered to advance south along the spur on which Government House stood and to secure the Jordanian village of Sur Behir, which dominated the road to Bethlehem. But the village was defended by two strongpoints, and although the Israelis gained a foothold in the village on the Monday night, they were driven out by a Jordanian counterattack. Next morning the Israelis returned to the offensive and during the course of the morning the Sur Bahir ridge was slowly and painfully cleared. Then, at noon, another Israeli battalion, supported by a company of Shermans, crashed through the barbed wire fence of the 1948 Armistice Line between

Government House and Mount Zion to clear the warren of houses forming the Abu Tur district of Jerusalem proper. Progress was slow, the house-to-house fighting was bitter, and the advancing Israelis came under increasing mortar fire from the Old City. By 7pm a small area near the Pool of Siloam had been cleared but casualties were such that Narkiss decided to pull the battalion back to Abu Tur.

While Narkiss's armour was rolling up the heights towards Ramallah another Israeli *Ugda* swung into action against the northern section of the Jordanian front. Commanded by Brigadier Elad Peled, Director of Israel's National Defence College, this *Ugda* of one armoured brigade, one infantry brigade and a number of independent infantry units, had been formed to deal with any hostile moves by the Syrians. When it was clear that Syria was not going to attack anywhere and that Jordan presented the more immediate and important threat, Peled was given fresh orders. While a battalion of infantry created a diversion by marching southwards from Tirat Tsvi along a track on the west side of the Jordan River, two separate armoured columns set off from Megiddo (in Israel) crossed the border at Moshav Ramon and headed for Jenin. A battery of the 'Long Toms' which had been shelling Tel Aviv was overrun en route, and at 3am on the Tuesday morning (the second day) the Israeli armour closed in on Jenin.

Within minutes the Israeli Shermans were halted by a battalion of Jordanian Pattons concealed in the olive groves round the town and waiting for them. The Israelis quickly recovered and a second assault was attempted. But when this failed they decided to try a ruse. Turning, the Shermans moved slowly back the way they had come, leaving their disabled vehicles behind, and leading the Jordanians to the conclusion that the Israelis were withdrawing. Breaking cover the Pattons gave chase. This was a fatal mistake, which ended with the virtual annihilation of the whole Jordanian battalion. Once this tank battle had been resolved the Israelis turned back to Jenin, and although the Jordanians fought hard the town was in Israeli hands by 7.30am.

About this time, however, Israeli aircraft reported about sixty Jordanian Pattons approaching Jenin from the south-east along the Nablus road. These were, in fact, two battalions of the 40th Jordanian Armoured Brigade returning to their former position after a fruitless journey to Jericho to relieve the 60th Brigade. To counter this sudden new threat the Israeli tanks had to go back through Jenin before they could turn south, and when the inhabitants saw this happening, they assumed that the Israelis were withdrawing. White flags fluttering from the windows of houses were hastily pulled in, rifles, machine guns and bazookas which had been concealed during the Israeli advance reappeared and the shooting flared up. This second round of fighting temporarily made life difficult for the Israelis who were trying to get out to meet the approaching Pattons. But the Israeli infantry who were left behind systematically broke this resistance, and by 1pm the shooting had been quelled and the town of Jenin was quiet.

Meanwhile Peled's Shermans had met the Jordanian Pattons, which were advancing in two columns – the first being fifteen miles ahead of the second. When the first Pattons spotted the Israeli Shermans they sheered off the road and deployed in positions they had occupied previously in the Kabatiya Hills. The Israelis charged on, only to run into an ambush staged by the second lot of Pattons, in which seventeen Shermans were destroyed. Reforming, the remaining Shermans turned to charge through the ambush and suffered more casualties. Two

Left and below: **Israeli Sherman tanks in action against Jordanian Pattons on the Jenin front**

Israeli air strikes were launched during the afternoon but they failed to dislodge the Jordanians and when night fell the tanks of both sides still faced each other across a valley dominated by the Kabatiya Hills. Next day, however, when the overwhelming power of the Israeli Air Force was put to use, the Israelis' fortunes changed. For eighteen hours, wave after wave of Mystères and Mirages skimmed over the battlefield between Jenin and Nablus or dived into the valley of the River Jordan beyond. Rockets and napalm rained down on the Jordanians and after eight hours the resistance was broken. The battle for Jerusalem had not been resolved by Wednesday afternoon (the third day) but Jordan was already beaten. The whole of the West Bank was as good as in Israeli hands and the famous Arab Legion had almost ceased to exist. At 1.30pm King Hussein told his troops that Jordan would continue to fight 'to the last breath and last drop of blood'. But the Security Council's call for a cease-fire was now his only chance of holding his crumbling nation together.

Before turning back to the sequence of events in Jerusalem, brief mention must be made of the capture of Latrun, the strategic village between the coastal plain and the inland mountains. The terra cotta roof of the massive stone Trappist monastery at Latrun can be seen for miles. This was built in 1890 next to a Crusader fortress, the Touron de Chevaliers, which had been built to guard the road to Jerusalem; the village stands on a little rise above the monastery. Near the top of a Jordanian salient which jutted into Israel, Latrun was on the old Jerusalem-Tel Aviv road, twenty miles from Tel Aviv and fifteen from Jerusalem. In 1948 the Latrun defile constituted the gateway to Jerusalem and it had witnessed

Israeli armour moves into the captured town of Jenin

some desperate fighting. Because the Israelis had repeatedly failed to capture the defile they had had to re-route a twenty mile stretch of road to Jerusalem round the Judean foothills and for nineteen years the old road was barred with a sign 'Stop. Frontier.' So Latrun was a place of bitter Israeli memories and its capture on Tuesday afternoon (the second day) by an Israeli infantry brigade a prestige gain. There was little more than token resistance and most of the Jordanian garrison withdrew. Fanning out from Latrun the Israelis cleared the salient during Wednesday morning, and an armoured column drove east towards Ramallah. That the Jordanians still had teeth and were prepared to use them was evident when the Israeli column ran into a road block, which was taken only after a brisk battle. Once this obstacle had been cleared, however, the Israeli infantry from Latrun were able to drive on and by late afternoon they had linked up with Narkiss's armoured brigade holding the Ramallah road junction. The setting for the vital battle of Jerusalem was now complete.

The inhabitants of Jerusalem were still in the shelters. News of Israeli victories in Sinai were beginning to percolate into the shelters of New Jerusalem, although Radio Damascus was still ranting about the 'hour of revenge' and exhorting 'Arab brothers' to 'get on to Tel Aviv'. But Radio Cairo and Radio Amman were less belligerent now, for defeatism had begun to set in at the headquarters of the UAR and Jordanian High Command. Shells and mortar bombs continued to fall in Jerusalem, however, and bursts of machine-gun fire swept the streets near the walls of the Old City when Narkiss issued his order for a night attack to seize the Mount Scopus Ridge from which the Israelis would be able to look down on the Holy City.

The 27th Infantry Brigade of the Arab Legion were manning the formidable concrete and stone emplacements along the 1948 Armistice Line. In front of these defences a wide stretch of open ground had been literally strewn with mines and other obstacles. Bangalore torpedos and explosive charges were used to clear paths, but the Israeli infantry suffered heavy casualties in the process. And once through the minefield they were plunged into desperate hand-to-hand fighting for the strong points which lay behind. Every yard of communication trench was contested, and when once these had been cleared there still remained the houses in which the retreating Jordanian troops took

Israeli tanks form up for the attack on Jerusalem

refuge and fought back. This was the biggest and fiercest infantry battle of the whole war; casualties were heavy on both sides, and it was here that the Arabs inflicted the worst damage on the Israelis.

Perhaps the toughest nut to crack of all the Jordanian defensive positions was Ammunition Hill, near the Police Training School. This was held by about 200 of the Arab Legion and the five-hour battle to evict them is generally acknowledged to be the fiercest engagement in all the Arab-Israeli operations so far. There were no glorious charges by tanks here – Mordechai Gur's paratroopers who took the position had to fight from bunker to bunker. And when they emerged from the maze of trenches, battered but triumphant, Ammunition Hill had cost them about fifty dead and three times as many wounded. Behind them lay 106 dead Jordanians, and every man of the remainder of the garrison wounded.

The paratroopers' task was not completed yet. The Police School stood at the entrance to the warren of houses known as the Sheikh Jarrah district, which for nineteen years had threatened the northern suburbs of New Jerusalem and cut off the road to the Mount Scopus enclave. More bloody house-to-house fighting took place before it was overrun. Meantime more of Gur's paratroopers had crossed the Armistice Line near the Mandelbaum Gate – the UN-controlled 'gate' between Israel and Jordan. In two columns the sweating paratroopers systematically battered their way through the buildings of the district known as the American Colony. Progress was slow, but it would have been slower still without the support of the artillery, tanks and Israeli aircraft which were called to assist. Two searchlights mounted on the tall Histradut building in New Jerusalem were used to indicate targets at night, and by day the Israelis hung flags from the buildings they had captured to show the limits of their advance. Houses that could not be overwhelmed by infantry firepower were dealt with at point-blank range by Shermans, and covered lanes were blasted through the houses for the evacuation of casualties and replenishment of ammunition.

With the capture of Sheikh Jarrah and the American Colony districts there came a lull in the fighting, broken only by the occasional sniper's shot or the explosion of a grenade. The Jordanians, soldiers and civilians alike, had evacuated the streets and houses outside the walls of the Old City and fled eastwards. For the Israelis who badly needed a breathing space to rest and replenish the relative calm was a welcome respite. It did not last long; from behind Jerusalem's ramparts the Arab Legion rallied and returned to the battle. From the high walls of the Old City Jordanian snipers picked off Israeli troops, and any movement which could be seen from the walls attracted a barrage of mortar and artillery fire from weapons sited on the Augusta Victoria Ridge behind the Mount of Olives. So the paratroops, who by now had reached the Rockefeller Museum, were ordered into action again.

The first attack was a failure. As the paratroops advanced across the open ground towards their objective, the Augusta Victoria Ridge, they were met with a hail of mortar bombs and small fire arms fire. They could not move, and the Sherman tanks which attempted to force a passage forwards were driven back to the shelter of the built up area by accurate and effective Jordanian anti-tank fire, bazookas fired from the Old City wall and guns located on the ridge. When two air strikes on the ridge failed to silence these guns Narkiss decided to wait until dusk and the attack was called off. The second attack was no more successful. Within minutes of the Shermans' crossing the start-line three of them had been knocked out, and casualties among the paratroopers were mounting at an alarming rate. So Narkiss again called off the attack; he would wait, he decided, until 11pm. By that time he would be able to organize and co-ordinate a more powerful assault.

In the event the attack never took place, for in this particular sector things did not now seem to be going so well for the Israelis. Heavy fighting had brought them considerable gains, and the Old City was virtually surrounded. But the failure to seize the Augusta Victoria Ridge was a distinct set-back, and there was some reason to suppose that the Jordanians were preparing for a counterattack down the Jericho road. To the Jordanians, however, the situation looked very different and any pessimism in Jerusalem was more than matched by gloom in Amman. Literally nothing had gone as King Hussein and General Riad had planned. The first brigade of Iraqi reinforcements which was to take over from the Arab Legion in the Jordan Valley had been spotted by the Israeli Air Force and bombed to pieces on its journey across the border. Three other brigades had been promised but by the time they reached Jordan's border President Aref realized the war was not going well for the Arabs, and his three brigades were ordered to halt. The Syrians had also failed Jordan; they had no air cover, they said. And the Egyptians, with problems enough of their own, were far from helpful. After talking to his master, Field-Marshal Amer, in Cairo, General Riad told Hussein that there seemed to be only two courses of action open: to ask the Israelis for a cease-fire, or to pull the Arab Legion back across the Jordan.

For Hussein these alternatives were too terrible to contemplate at first. Unlike other Arab politicians – and most Egyptian generals – the King had spent much of the war in the forward areas, racing from one unit to another urging his troops to hold their ground. Nasser had called him 'a traitor to the Arabs' before the war, and he did not wish to lend substance to this accusation by being the first Arab leader to sue for peace. Nor did he wish to abandon the West Bank, which he might never recover. (Arab jealousies die hard and no doubt Hussein harboured a suspicion that some of his Arab allies would not be sorry to see the richest part of his kingdom lopped off – even by the Israelis). Early on the Tuesday morning (the second day) Hussein had his famous conversation with Nasser about foreign intervention. At 1.30pm he told his troops that Jordan would fight on; yet within half an hour he had come to accept the conclusions of the Egyptian commander-in-chief of his forces and started to think about a cease-fire. Meantime Riad was working on the basis of the King's determination to fight on, and at 10pm he issued an order for all Jordanian forces to pull back to the East Bank. About half an hour after this the UN called for a cease-fire, and although the Jordanians chose to ignore this particular appeal its effect was coupled with the withdrawal order. As it looked as if there might be some advantage in the Arab Legion staying where it was, Riad's order was countermanded, and Jordanian units ordered to stand fast if they had not moved or to go back if they had. Order, counter-order, disorder: in several places the Arab Legionnaires had to fight to get back to the positions they had evacuated; in others the countermanding order did not reach the units concerned until it was too late. This is what happened in Jerusalem, where two battalions packed up and slipped away during the night. Finally in the early hours of Wednesday morning Hussein called on his troops to obey the UN cease-fire, provided the Israelis did the same. It was at this point that the morale of the bewildered and long-suffering Legionnaires began to falter. Because they were moving in accordance with the order to withdraw or the second order to go back, it was a

The infantry begins its attack on the Old City

long time before the order to stop shooting reached them. In any case the UN appeal could not have been effective because the Israelis had chosen to ignore it until they had occupied their ancient capital and regained the most vital landmark of their existence, the Wailing Wall.

Not knowing that the greater part of the Jordanian garrison of the Old City were pulling out the Israelis spent Tuesday night licking their wounds and waiting for a counter-attack which never materialized. Next morning, however, when the pilot of an Israeli aircraft making a dawn reconnaissance reported seeing troops and traffic moving away from Jerusalem and none towards it, Narkiss ordered a resumption of the offensive. Preceded by an artillery barrage and an air strike, Gur's paratroops again assaulted the Augusta Victoria Ridge. Apart from a token rearguard, which fled downhill as the Israelis approached, the ridge was deserted. Most of the Jordanians had left before dawn and when the paratroops swept south to take the El Tur district and the Mount of Olives they met only scattered opposition. So, once these areas had been secured and the Jerusalem-Jericho road blocked, Gur assembled his force for an attack on the Old City from the east.

In the early heat of the Mediterranean sun a battalion of paratroopers followed a section of Shermans down the Jericho road towards St Stephen's Gate, known to the Israelis as the 'Lion's Gate'. There they stopped for what was to be the final assault, while mortar fire was put down on the Moslem Quarter near the gate and recoilless guns blasted the ramparts. Over the intercom radio in his half-track, Gur, speaking in a voice charged with emotion announced: '. . . we are about to take the Temple Mount. This is an historic task. The Jewish people are praying for our

Above and below: Arabs surrender to advancing Israeli forces. Their Israeli captors suspect some of them of being Jordanian soldiers in civilian clothes. *Below right:* One of the Israelis' first wave of assault troops, impatient to get to the Wailing Wall, is hit in the chest by an Arab bullet. He died shortly afterwards

victory. All of Israel is waiting for it . . . I wish you success . . .' Then roaring up to St Stephen's Gate Gur's vehicle charged through into the Old City. The nail studded door of the Gate had been damaged by a shell and it collapsed as he drove through. Turning left Gur headed towards the Temple Mount, with his paratroops running behind. It is 150 yards from the St Stephen's Gate to the majestic Mosque of the Dome of the Rock. The Israelis covered the distance in minutes, dodging in and out among the ancient olive and pine trees covering the crest of Mt Morjah, the Temple Mount. As they ran, bullets fired by Arab Legionnaires manning a post behind the Al-Aksa Mosque sang past them. But the sole remaining battalion of Jordanian troops had slipped away through a gap in the Israeli ring while the paratroops were forming up for their attack.

The first paratroops reached the Wailing Wall about 10.15am, and soon after that the Governor of what had been Arab Jerusalem approached Gur in the Temple Square. The Jordanian troops had left, he declared, and resistance would cease. Meantime the paratroops were making sure that there would be no more shooting. As they fanned out to search and occupy the Old City, loudspeakers summoned the survivors to come from their homes and surrender. But bullets were still flying when the Chief Rabbi of the Israeli Army, Brigadier Shlomo Goren, arrived at the wall to lead an ecstatic gathering of sweating paratroopers and government ministers in prayer. Holding his Scrolls of the Law in his left hand, and a ram's horn brought to Israel by a survivor of Belsen in his right hand, the Chief Rabbi solemnly sounded a call for rejoicing. For many Israelis it would not have mattered now if the war had gone no further, for this act signified complete victory. What was happening in Sinai was more sensational and

Above: Rabbi Shlomo Goren, with the Scrolls of the Law and ram's horn, arrives at the Wailing Wall on 7th June. *Below:* Jewish soldiers and civilians offer prayers on their people's return to the Wailing Wall. *Right:* General Dayan, Brigadier Narkiss (left) and General Rabin enter the Old City at Lion's Gate

certainly far more important militarily than the capture of the Holy City. But the Wailing Wall had symbolised Jewish national hopes for 1,897 years, and the Israelis' attitude was summed up by Gur when he stood before its great boulders: 'None of us alive has ever seen or done anything so great as he has done today.'

General Dayan was among the first Israeli VIPs to contemplate the ancient stones of the Second Temple. Troops beside him, carefully cradling rifles and bazookas under their arms, stood with heads bowed as he offered up an intransigent prayer: 'We have returned to the most sacred of our shrines never to part from them again.'

If Dayan believed in divine providence for the fulfilment of the 2,000-year dream, events to the north of Jerusalem had already established that he was not leaving Jordan's defeat entirely to the Almighty. By the early hours of Wednesday morning Peled's armour was poised for an assault on Nablus. Pattons of the Jordanian 40th Armoured Brigade and men of the 25th Infantry Brigade blocking the road south from Jenin were routed and scattered at Kufeir, by a combined air and tank assault in an operation which was a textbook demonstration of the modern and bloody employment of air power. As the Pattons withdrew they were picked off individually by Israeli aircraft. Akkaba and Tubas were taken without opposition and the Israeli tanks roamed on south to the junction of the road leading from Damya Bridge to Nablus. Here the column divided, one armoured battalion driving south into the Jordan Valley while the remainder of the brigade turned towards Nablus. At the outskirts of the town they received an unexpected welcome. The war had moved too quickly for the inhabitants of Nablus. Peace and quiet prevailed in the town and the Israeli tanks were mistaken for those of the Iraqis who had been expected to pass through on their triumphant march to Tel Aviv. When the real identity of the visitors became apparent and the true situation dawned, however, the cheering stopped and the townsfolk dispersed to lock themselves in their houses. Sniping started, and it was several hours before Israeli infantrymen finally nailed down control of the town.

Peled's armour did not stay to see this operation completed. From Nablus the Israeli tanks headed west along the road to Deir Sharaf and Nathanya. Israeli aircraft had seen Jordanian Pattons, retreating from the previous day's action below Jenin, moving south along the road from Arraba. When the two forces clashed a tank battle ensued in which Israeli AMXs knocked out ten Pattons at close range. The Israeli Air Force which joined in claimed another fifteen more. With this action on the Thursday morning the fighting in the northern sector came to a complete stop. At Damya Bridge the Israeli tanks stood back from the river bank to allow hordes of fearful refugees and disorganized bands of Arab Legionnaires to cross unimpeded to the East Bank. All the Jordanians were on foot by this time as Israeli aircraft attacked any vehicle identified as Jordanian with rocket - and cannon-fire or napalm.

South and east of Jerusalem other Biblical towns fell to the advancing Israelis – Bethlehem, Hebron, Jericho – until they had seized all of Hussein's kingdom west of the Jordan River and the Dead Sea. As in Sinai Israel's absolute mastery of the air meant ultimate Arab defeat. On Thursday morning (the fourth day) Hussein, unshaven and hollow-eyed, returned sadly to Amman to announce that his men could fight no longer, and to send a message to U Thant telling him that Jordan would accept a cease-fire.

New regime in Old Jersualem; Israeli troops mount guard on the Holy Places

הכניסה לזרים אסורו
HOLY PLACE
THORISED ENTRY IS FORBIDDEN
BY ORDER

The conquests continue: Dayan and army chiefs visit Bethlehem (above) and Hebron (below)

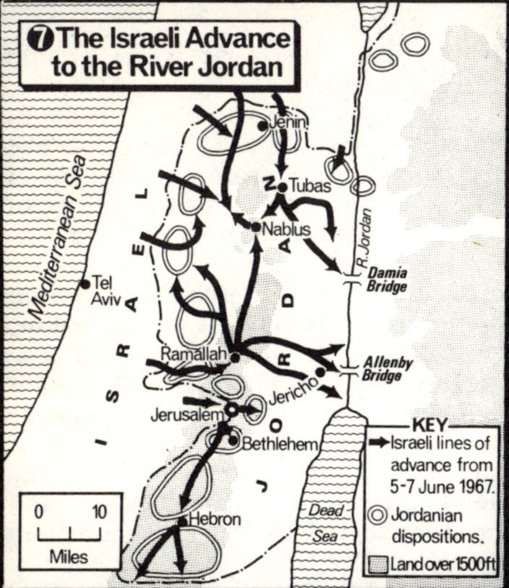

7 The Israeli Advance to the River Jordan
Jenin
Tubas
Nablus
R. Jordan
Damia Bridge
Mediterranean Sea
Tel Aviv
ISRAEL
JORDAN
Ramallah
Allenby Bridge
Jericho
Jerusalem
Bethlehem
Hebron
Dead Sea
KEY
Israeli lines of advance from 5-7 June 1967.
Jordanian dispositions.
Land over 1500ft
0 10
Miles

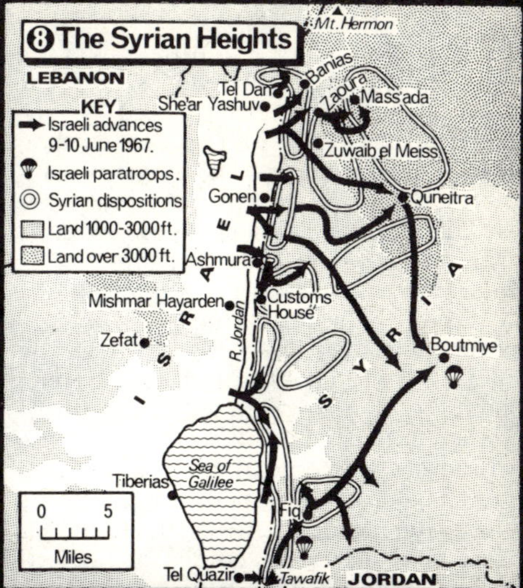

8 The Syrian Heights
Mt. Hermon
LEBANON
Banias
Tel Dan
She'ar Yashuv
Zaoura
Mass'ada
KEY
Israeli advances 9-10 June 1967.
Israeli paratroops.
Syrian dispositions
Land 1000-3000 ft.
Land over 3000 ft.
Zuwaib el Meiss
Gonen
Quneitra
Ashmura
Mishmar Hayarden
Customs House
Zefat
R. Jordan
ISRAEL
SYRIA
Boutmiye
Sea of Galilee
Tiberias
Fiq
0 5
Miles
Tel Quazir
Tawafik
JORDAN

The Northern Front

In New York on Wednesday evening (the third day) delegates of the United Nations were treated to the curious spectacle of the Soviet Ambassador urgently presenting a resolution calling for an absolute cease-fire in the Middle East by 8pm GMT. It was already too late to save Egypt, but Moscow was anxious to stop the war before Israeli troops could consolidate Sharm El Sheikh. Unless the Israelis could be halted and driven back the Arabs would suffer a humiliating defeat. Israel said that she would cease fire if all the Arab states did the same, but 8pm came and went with the combatants still fighting. And next day the combatants continued to pound each other in defiance of the UN mandatory order. In Sinai the Israelis were fighting the crucial battles to block the Egyptian escape routes to the Suez Canal, and in Jordan the fighting had also reached its climax. In the north there was little fighting but Radio Damascus was still ranting about 'hoisting the Palestinian flag in the skies of Tel Aviv'.

Overnight the Syrians' attitude seemed to change, since they agreed to a cease-fire on Thursday morning: when Egypt followed suit a few hours later it looked as if the war was over. But it was not. The Israelis had a long standing and bitter score to settle with their northern neighbours. For years Syria had maintained a constant stream of abuse and propaganda against Israel; invented the slogan of the 'Popular Liberation War'; recruited, armed, trained and financed the Palestinian guerillas and then sent them into Israel to burn, wreck, ruin and destroy. It was Syria who had been the cause of the war, and the Israelis intended that Syria should pay for its sins.

The border between the two countries ran north-south, and stretched for twenty miles from the kibbutz of Tel Dan in the north to the shores of lake Galilee in the south. On the Syrian side a slope rose steeply to a crest some three miles away, which dominated the Israeli plain below. Over the years the Syrians had constructed a strongly fortified belt of defences, ten miles deep. 265 guns were dug into the hills behind the crest, and the infantry positions on the height itself were concreted and interconnected with underground trenches. The front itself was heavily mined and anti-tank guns were sited in depth. These forward defences were manned by three infantry brigades, each supported by T-34s and SU-100s. Scattered among the front line defences there were also thirty German Panzer tanks of Second World War vintage, and some 75mm guns. A week or two before the war started three other infantry brigades were sent up to reinforce the defences. All in all, on 5th June there were over 40,000 Syrian soldiers with 260 tanks and self-propelled guns in three armoured brigades and five infantry brigades on the Golan Plateau. Tactically they were in a very strong position. But it was an inefficient army which was preparing to drive the Jews into the sea. Vehicles were badly maintained, weapons were filthy and there was no sanitary discipline in the fixed defences. The Russian advisers and instructors, who had come to teach the Syrians how to use the sophisticated armaments which the Soviet Union had provided, were exasperated.

On 5th June (the first day) the northern front was unusually quiet, and the only evidence of Syrian hostility was a bomb dropped by Syrian aircraft on the little town of Tiberias (before the Israeli Air Force struck at Syria's air bases). But early in the morning of the second day of the war – encouraged perhaps by Radio Cairo's false claims of successes in the south – the Syrians put down a heavy artillery barrage on the frontier kibbutzim at Shear Yusuv and Tel Dan. When the barrage lifted about 7am two companies of Syrian infantry crossed the border under cover of fire from tanks on the Banias Ridge above Tel Dan with the obvious intention of enclosing the settlement in a pincer movement. The attack was held up by Israeli militia – farmers, shopkeepers, the local bus driver, and when Israeli aircraft arrived on the scene at 7.20am their cannon fire and napalm induced the invaders to beat a quick retreat.

Throughout the second, third and fourth days of the war the Syrians intermittently bombarded all the Israeli settlements within range of their guns – from Kibbutz Dan and Kfar Szold in the north, through Gadot and Rosh Pina in the middle, to Ein Ger, Haon and Tel Kazir in the south. There were casualties, but most of the Israeli farmers stayed in their shelters and most of the damage caused by the shelling was to their crops.

Syria's agreement to a cease-fire on Thursday morning (the fourth day) brought a five hour lull in the shelling. Then it started again and Radio Damascus announced that Syria was not bound by any cease-fire. Believing that they were holding impregnable positions, the Syrians were emboldened by the fact that the Israelis had not attempted to attack. Israel's troops had overstretched themselves on the southern and central front they calculated. Furthermore they reckoned that Israel would not wish to further provoke the Soviet Union. But the Syrians were wrong. Israel's army still had the power to deal with Syria, and was more than keen to do so. The Israeli cabinet was divided on the issue, and there was a good case for holding off an attack. A proposal had been received from the Russians that if Israel would let Syria off the hook, then the Soviet Union might allow to emigrate those of Russia's three million Jews who wished to do so. It was bait, bribe, and blood money. But it was a cogent reason for leaving Syria alone. After a long argument however, the Israeli cabinet decided that the Russians could not be trusted, and that Israel might never again be presented with the opportunity to sweep away the menace of the formidable Syrian Western Wall. Israeli troops must show the Syrians that even with Russian advice, guidance and equipment, Israel could overcome them.

Orders went out to that effect at about 6pm Jerusalem time, and Israeli troops began to concentrate for the offensive. In the north two of the armoured brigades which had been fighting the Jordanians as part of the Peled *Ugda*, and the paratroop brigade which had been in action with Uzi Narkiss were put under command of Brigadier David Elazar. The infantry brigade which had made a feint move south into Jordan on the Tuesday and which had reassembled south of the Sea of Galilee was also put under Elazar's command. So too was one of the last of the reserve brigades which had not yet seen any action and which had concentrated near Givat Haem in the north. The three mechanized infantry battalions of the famous Golani brigade, commanded by Colonel Yona, and another infantry brigade completed the force which was to smash through the Syrian defences. Its total strength amounted to about 250 tanks – almost as many as the Syrians – and about 20,000 men.

Elazar's orders were simple. The Syrian armour was to be drawn into battle, the Golan plateau was to be seized and the artillery which had

Brigadier David Elazar

Israeli Shermans go into the attack on the Golan Heights

harassed the Israelis for the past two years was to be destroyed. The road to Damascus was to be forced open to show the Syrians that topographical advantage did not guarantee their immunity. Once these objectives were accomplished the offensive would stop; in victory Israel would demonstrate magnanimity.

The Israeli plan was bold but extremely conventional. The attack was to be made on four fronts, the main thrust being directed against the northern sector, where the terrain was hardest and the Syrian position least strongly defended. The Golani brigade, which, with two companies of Shermans, was designated for this task, was given Banias Ridge as its objective. Still in the northern sector but slightly south of the Golani brigade's operation one of the armoured brigades starting from Kfar Szold would force a passage through the first line of Syrian defences to seize Zaoura. It would then turn south-west and smash its way through the second and third lines of Syrian positions to seize the town of Kuneitra, where the Syrians had their headquarters. These attacks were complementary. In the centre sector one of the armoured brigades which had returned from Jordan was to attack towards Rawye, after a path had been cleared for the tanks by infantry. When the tanks went in the infantry would follow and exploit towards Dardara, a village on the lower road to Kuneitra. In the south central sector infantry would advance from Almagor and exploit down the eastern side of the Sea of Galilee. And finally, in the very south the paratroop brigade from Jerusalem would break into the Golan plateau near Tel Kazir. In all these operations the paramount aim was to seize Kuneitra.

The ground attacks were scheduled to start at 7am on Friday morning

Kuneitra

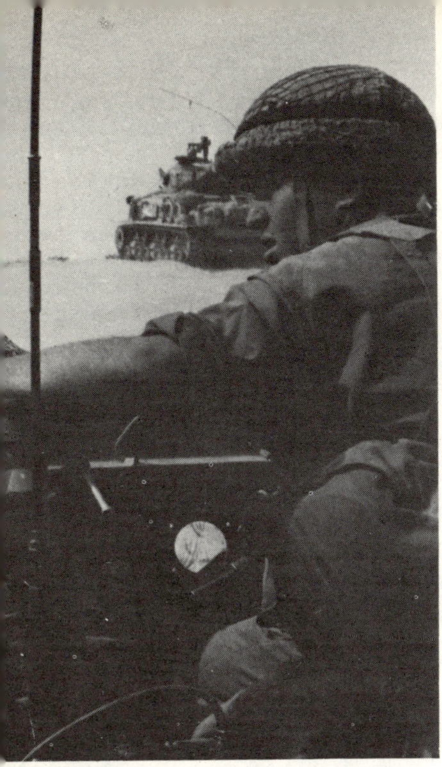

Armour advances on the Northern Front

(the fifth day), and from dawn that day until the final cease-fire came into effect at 6.30pm on Saturday Israeli aircraft pounded the Syrian positions. Their bombs did little damage to the concrete and stone emplacements, and the napalm which was dropped was channelled away in the gutters which the Syrians had providentially fixed to their overhead cover. But many of the defenders were stunned by the blast of bombs and their morale was shaken by the continuity and persistence of the Israeli strikes. Israeli sappers started to clear paths through the minefields before first light. Clearing lanes through their own minefields proved to be more difficult than the minefields of the Syrians. On this part of the border rains washed many mines away, necessitating the minefields being resown periodically. The Israelis had done this conscientiously, but the Syrians had not bothered, so there were great gaps in their minefield belt. In anticipation of their own advance to Tiberias and Tel Aviv, the Syrians had also lifted many of the mines they had sown round the Beni Yakov bridge across the Jordan.

The first Israeli formation to cross the Syrian border was the armoured brigade which mounted the heights in two columns from the vicinity of Kfar Szold. As they crossed the No Man's Land on the two sides of the frontier the Syrian artillery laid down a heavy barrage and although the Israeli Air Force screamed down on these guns the men and vehicles suffered many casualties. At the border eight bulldozers went into the lead to clear the mines which the sappers had not been able to reach; five of these were knocked out before the armoured columns were through the minefield.

An Israeli machine-gun post, with a rifleman in support, in action against the Syrian defenders

Nine hours elapsed before the tanks reached the crest, and the Israelis took heavy casualties all the way. Meantime the Golani brigade did not cross the border until 2pm. The Syrian guns had created havoc in the initial phases of the attack and when the infantry did reach the first line of Syrian positions, the defenders were ousted only after bitter hand-to-hand combat inside the positions. Fortifications, such as those at Tel Azzaziat, had already acquired a notorious reputation from the many border incidents of the years before. The fights here lasted until 6.30pm and this battle is regarded with the battle for Ammunition Hill, as one of the two most hard fought and costly engagements of the whole war. When it was over sixty Syrians had been killed and twenty others captured; the cost to the Israelis was thirty killed and about seventy wounded.

About ten miles further south AMX tanks raced across the border about noon. They were not supported by infantry and they took the Syrians by surprise. By the time the latter could call down artillery support the tanks were already on their forward positions on the first crest of the

A Russian-supplied tank and other war vehicles knocked out in the Golan Heights area

plateau. Bulldozers and infantry came up in a second wave to clear a passage through the barbed wire and fashion a rough road passable for wheeled vehicles. Then the third wave went in, consisting of infantry in buses, lorries and furniture vans. Panicking, the Syrians radioed for tank support; in doing so the location of the tanks was disclosed to the Israelis who were monitoring the Syrian wave-lengths. The information was passed to the Israeli Air Force, and the Syrian tanks never arrived.

By Friday evening the Israelis had established a bridgehead five miles wide on the top of the Golan escarpment between Zaoura and Kala and had penetrated the northern part of the Syrian defensive wall in five other places. When night fell they were on the outskirts of Masada. But it had not been an easy day for the Israelis. They had not been as successful as they had hoped, and their programme was behind schedule. Organisational problems, preparation, reconnaissance, briefing and re-supply had all been more difficult than expected. So too had the terrain, and the Syrians had shown an unexpected resilience – generally standing fast and fighting back until their posts were physically over-run.

Throughout that night, the first with a full moon and for the Israelis

the Sabbath, Elazar's men regrouped and waited for a counterattack which never came, while helicopters landed in the forward areas and removed the wounded. At dawn the offensive was resumed in all four sectors of the front. From Zaoura and Rawye armoured columns set out for Kuneitra, while a third force headed south-east towards Boutmiya.

The Syrians put up a stiff resistance until about noon. Then their opposition began to crumble, and the Israelis took one position after another. From Banias in the north to Tawafik in the south the Syrian troops were throwing down their weapons and taking to their heels. Discipline had gone and the morale of the Syrian soldiers had disintegrated. The conflict had turned into a rout, as the Israeli armour set out in pursuit of the fleeing Syrians. Tanks and positions which had not been abandoned were destroyed en route, and at 2.30pm the Israelis entered Kuneitra. It was a ghost town where tanks had been abandoned with their engines running and their radios on. Leaving the mopping up operations to the infantry of the Golani brigade, the Israeli armour pushed on southward towards Boutmiya.

Meanwhile Syrian resistance in the south had also collapsed, and when the Israelis moved in to attack the fortified ridge stretching from Tawafik through Kfar Hareb to El Al at 2pm the defences were found to be empty. It appeared that the Syrian defeat was complete. However, as it was not known whether the villages and positions behind the defensive belt had been abandoned a rapid advance was called for. A helicopter was sent on to reconnoitre and when it reported that the entire Golan Heights appeared to have been abandoned a paratroop force was put into helicopters and set down at key points ahead of the tanks and infantry. As the tanks and infantry advanced over the rough terrain eastwards and north towards what was to become the cease-fire line, the helicopters leap-frogged the paratroops forward – until finally they landed at the deserted Boutmiya crossroads. Here at this junction there was a reunion of paratroops, tanks from Kuneitra, tanks from Dardara, tanks from Kfar Harib, and tanks and infantry from Tel Kazir.

By 6.30pm when the cease-fire came into effect the Israelis were in complete control of the Golan Heights and were driving round the deserted eastern shores of Lake Galilee as if they were on Dizengoff Road in the heart of Tel Aviv. The road to Damascus was open and at a cost of 152 killed and 306 wounded the Israelis had achieved all they had set out to achieve. The war was over.

War debris overlooking the Sea of Galilee

The war at sea

Israel's stupendous victory was won in the air over Egypt and on the battlefields of Sinai, Jerusalem and the Golan Heights. At sea the Israeli and Egyptian navies went into action, but their achievements were unspectacular and relatively uninfluential. Apart from landing a party of sailors at Sharm El Sheikh on Wednesday 7th June, Israeli naval operations were limited to two sorties against Egyptian naval bases and the interception of three submarines. A combined naval and air assault on El Arish, planned to take place on the first night of the war, was called off, partly because Jordan had joined battle, and partly because Tal's troops had done better than expected. Consequently the Israeli Navy had little chance to show its mettle and gain glory. With the Israeli Air Force, however, it could share the credit for the freedom from bombardment of Israel's long and vulnerable coastline throughout the course of hostilities.

As darkness fell on 5th June, an Israeli flotilla slipped down the Israeli coast and sailed along the shores of Sinai towards Port Said. The commander of the Israeli ships knew that the Egyptian Air Force had virtually ceased to exist, while the commander-in-chief of the Egyptian Navy, Rear-Admiral Soliman Izzat, was blissfully unaware of this fact. As the Egyptian High Command had not yet dared to reveal to Nasser the extent of the disaster, it is scarcely surprising that Izzat was left in ignorance. He had no reason to disbelieve the extravagant claims broadcast by Radio Cairo, and every reason therefore to be confident that the very existence of the Egyptian Air Force would deter offensive action in Egyptian waters by the Israeli Navy.

Consequently the Egyptians were not expecting the Israeli flotilla, which was within fifteen miles of Port Said before there was any Egyptian reaction. The Israelis then spotted two Osa Class patrol boats heading towards them at high speed. When the Egyptian vessels were less than a mile away and closing in rapidly, an Israeli destroyer opened fire. Several shots were seen to strike the patrol boats, which veered off, turned about, and made off into Port Said harbour.

This action was incidental to the Israeli main operation, which then continued. First at Port Said and later at Alexandria, two small parties of frogmen were put ashore with orders to do as much damage as possible to Egyptian naval vessels and installations. Four of the Osa patrol boats and three frigates were known to be in Port Said and the Israelis hoped to be able to put some, if not all of them, out of action. In the event the frogmen succeeded in getting into the harbour but were unable to find any of the ships they were looking for. A couple of laden oil tankers tempted them as alternative targets, but the Israelis decided that if they did blow them up, the resultant explosion would probably devastate not only the dock area but the town itself. So they slipped back to the rendezvous where boats were waiting to take them home. Their mission, efficiently performed but unspectacular because it did not achieve its objective, was not a success.

The other operation was more successful, but the men who took part

Israeli frogmen

were less fortunate. Taken by submarine to a point just off the Ras El Tin naval base, six Israeli frogmen rowed ashore in a small dinghy and successfully made their way into the main anchorage. There they damaged a number of vessels and sank several, among them a missile craft of the Osa class. With their task completed the frogmen then tried to return to the rendezvous where the submarine which had brought them to Alexandria was supposed to pick them up. Arriving late at the rendezvous, all six men had to lie up until the next night when the submarine would return if they had failed to turn up first time. According to the Israelis the submarine went back and waited on both nights, while the Egyptians claimed that they had detected the submarine soon after it had put the frogmen ashore and had fired on it. Hoping that it would return they had also had a naval force lying in wait, but the submarine failed to show up. In the event the six Israeli sailors were captured on Tuesday afternoon, and were eventually repatriated when the war ended.

Meantime the Israeli flotilla which took the frogmen to Port Said had withdrawn from Egyptian territorial waters. The Egyptian Air Force still had some serviceable aircraft, and Brigadier Erell did not want his ships to be caught napping. As soon as the Egyptians realized that the force blockading their harbour had gone, however, the ships which the frogmen had been looking for slipped away westward along the coast to Alexandria. Alexandria was a comparatively safe haven, but the Egyptian patrol boats were not in a position to sally out and bombard the Israeli coastline and sneak back to harbour without fear of retaliation. Their range was limited by the fuel they could carry, and refuelling at sea in daylight would make them sitting

Patrol boats of the Israeli navy seen in the Straits of Tiran

ducks for the Israeli Air Force. Only from Port Said was it possible for the Osas to reach Israel and return to base during the short hours of darkness.

On Wednesday and Thursday, the Israelis spotted submarines near Rosh Hanikra close to the Lebanese-Israeli border, and Haifa. Israeli destroyers attacked them and the submarines submerged. Oil slicks, which appeared on the surface later, were a sign that the submarines were damaged if not sunk. Perhaps the most interesting facet of the action off Haifa was the subsequent Egyptian denial that any of their submarines went anywhere near Haifa or the northern Israeli coast during hostilities.

Another mysterious casualty of the war was the American naval communications ship *USS Liberty*, a converted freighter crammed with electronic equipment. Chugging along at about five knots on a west-northwest

The Gulf of Aquaba. A helicopter hovers over a destroyed artillery emplacement

Patrol boat of the Israeli navy in the Straits of Tiran

course about twelve miles off the Sinai coast, the *Liberty* was sighted by two Israeli patrol boats on Thursday afternoon. Believing it to be an Egyptian vessel in disguise, the patrol boats commander reported their conclusion by radio and asked for air support. The message was duly passed to the Israeli operations room at Jerusalem, where all requests for air support were monitored and coordinated, and the patrol boats were told to take another look at the *Liberty* and confirm that it was an enemy ship. Yes, came the reply. It was probably the Egyptian supply ship *El Quesir* . . . but there was the possibility that it might be a Soviet vessel. Meanwhile the United States and Soviet embassies in Tel Aviv were asked if they had any ships operating in the area where the suspect vessel had been sighted; both said that they

The 'technical research' ship USS *Liberty*, showing the damage from strafing runs and the torpedo hole in her side

did not.

So a strike was authorized and shortly after 2pm three Mirages took off to home on the *Liberty*. Sweeping across the ship's starboard bow they raked the American vessel with machine gun and cannon fire, riddling its hull and superstructure in half a dozen strafing runs. When the planes flew off the waiting Israeli patrol boats closed in. Making for the *Liberty* with all machine-guns firing, they launched two torpedoes. One of these found its mark and tore a gaping hole in the *Liberty* squarely amidships and below the water line. Thirty-five minutes later the Israeli attack ended as abruptly as it had begun. The flag at the *Liberty's* masthead had been shot away during the strafing runs, but the patrol boats had got close enough to see the English lettering on the ship's stern and the 'holding ensign' that had been run up to replace the lost flag.

Once they had realized their mistake the Israeli patrol boat commanders stopped astern of the *Liberty* to signal 'Do you need assistance', and when they radioed the news back to the shore an Israeli helicopter was put at the disposal of the United States naval attache. He flew out to the *Liberty* but was refused permission to go aboard and flew back to Tel Aviv after dropping his visiting card on the deck of the stricken ship. Refusing all offers of Israeli assistance, the captain of the *Liberty*, Commander William McConagle, patched up the hole in the side of his ship and steamed away north. The *Liberty* was listing heavily to starboard but its watertight compartments kept it afloat. In due course it was joined by the cruiser *USS Little Rock* which escorted the *Liberty* into Malta where it was put into dry dock for repairs.

Thirty-four officers and men of the *Liberty* crew were killed and seventy others wounded in this action. And as might be expected there was a storm of controvery about the incident. Israel offered an apology and full compensation, claiming that it had mistaken the ship for an Egyptian vessel. The United States accepted the apology but a secret court of inquiry was set up to investigate. Why a sophisticated American 'spy ship' should be cruising so close to the battle zone was a question which has never been publicly answered. In the absence of official explanations theories proliferated. Perhaps the

most interesting, if not most outrageous, of these was that the Israelis attacked the *Liberty* because she had monitored communications proving that Israel had started the war. Another maintained that the ship's American flag was seen before the Mirages commenced their attack, but it was thought to be an Arab ruse.

Ironically, the court of inquiry reported that on the morning of the attack the United States Joint Chiefs of Staff had ordered the *Liberty* to move further away from the coast 'even though such a move would partially degrade her mission' – whatever it was. Moreover only three days earlier the Israelis had asked the Pentagon what ships it would have in the area in the coming week. Because of some mix-up they got no reply; which lent credence to their later belief that no United States ships were operating in the area and that the *Liberty* must therefore be an Egyptian ship flying an American flag in order to get close to bombard El Arish, which had been captured by the Israelis. The only clear facts about this mysterious episode were the grim casualty figures.

Aftermath

Egypt finally accepted the United Nations Security Council's call for a cease-fire on Thursday evening 8th June, and President Nasser delivered a radio and television address to the Arab world on 9th June. He had made no public utterance since the beginning of the war. The only official voice had been Radio Cairo, broadcasting the optimistic communiques of the UAR High Command and the fatuous rhetoric of commentators who were still boasting of Arab victories at a time when the Egyptian army was no longer capable of defending the Suez Canal and the road to Cairo was open. The Arabs could have learned the truth from foreign radio stations, but until the remnants of the Egyptian army began to find their way home, the Egyptian public did not begin to grasp the full extent of the disaster. So when Nasser announced the cease-fire after his long silence, the news came as a shock. People were angry and bewildered by the fact that the army appeared to have given up so soon. Despite the accusations of American and British air support for the Israelis there was not the excuse of 1956 that Egypt had had to face an attack of two great powers as well as Israel.

It was Nasser's darkest hour, for the defeat was far worse than in 1956. Israeli troops had not only occupied the whole of Sinai but also held the east bank of the Suez Canal for which Egypt had run such risks to regain control and had made such efforts to develop. Egypt's allies had collapsed, and Nasser's work of fifteen years – ousting foreign troops from Egypt, establishing control of the Suez Canal, and restoring self-confidence among

The Suez canal is blocked by the hulks of shipping destroyed during the fighting

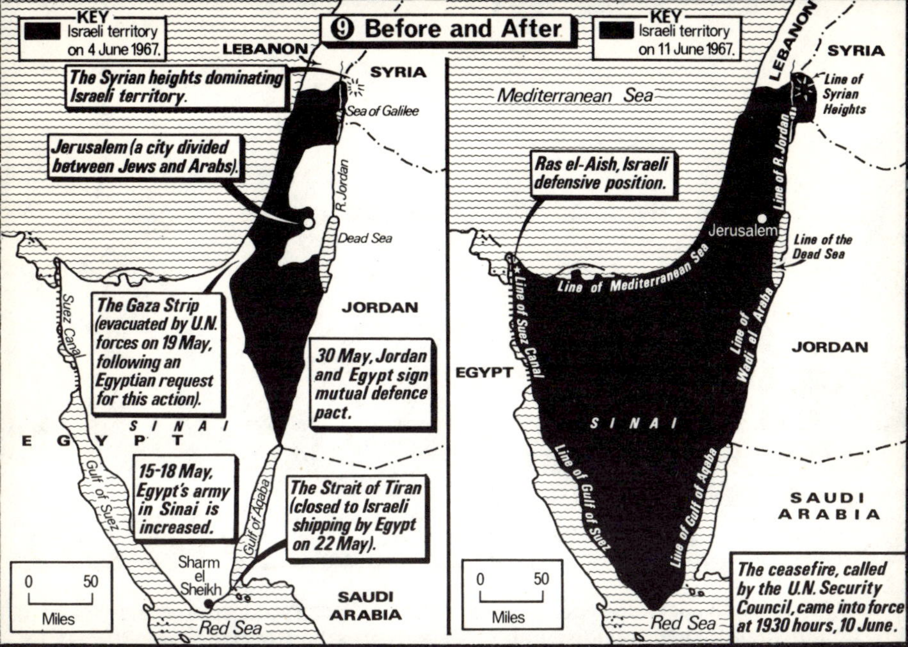

9 Before and After
KEY
Israeli territory on 4 June 1967.
LEBANON
SYRIA
The Syrian heights dominating Israeli territory.
Sea of Galilee
Jerusalem (a city divided between Jews and Arabs).
R. Jordan
Dead Sea
Suez Canal
The Gaza Strip (evacuated by U.N. forces on 19 May, following an Egyptian request for this action).
JORDAN
30 May, Jordan and Egypt sign mutual defence pact.
SINAI
EGYPT
Gulf of Suez
15-18 May, Egypt's army in Sinai is increased.
Gulf of Aqaba
The Strait of Tiran (closed to Israeli shipping by Egypt on 22 May).
Sharm el Sheikh
SAUDI ARABIA
Red Sea
0 50
Miles
KEY
Israeli territory on 11 June 1967.
LEBANON
SYRIA
Line of Syrian Heights
Mediterranean Sea
Ras el-Aish, Israeli defensive position.
Line of R. Jordan
Jerusalem
Line of the Dead Sea
Line of Mediterranean Sea
Line of Suez Canal
Line of Wadi el Araba
EGYPT
JORDAN
SINAI
Line of Gulf of Suez
Line of Gulf of Aqaba
SAUDI ARABIA
The ceasefire, called by the U.N. Security Council, came into force at 1930 hours, 10 June.
0 50
Miles
Red Sea

A weary President Nasser goes on television to announce his resignation

the Arab world – all seemed to have been brought to ruin in a few disastrous days. Now the Arab world faced the prospects of a humiliating capitulation, for there was no hope as in 1956 of snatching diplomatic victories from military defeat. World opinion was no longer overwhelmingly on Egypt's side as it had been in 1956.

The pre-war picture of Israel as a beleaguered fortress, threatened by a ring of hostile Arab armies bent not only on her defeat but the actual annihilation of her people had earned the Israelis wide international sympathy, especially in Europe and the United States. In other countries too, in Asia, Africa, Latin America and even within the Communist countries of Eastern Europe, there was now greater sympathy for the Israelis who were deemed to have hit back only after unreasonable provocation. Moreover, by the discrepancies between their threats and their performance, the Arabs had invited world derision. Over the centuries the Jews have learned to extract a laugh from almost any event, tribulation or triumph. By the end of the war people were chuckling over jokes about the Israeli 'blitzkrieg', in which a crack regiment known as the Bagel Lancers had taken part. In the *New York Times* a full-page advertisement recommended *Visit Israel And See The Pyramids*. Unofficial humour of this nature added lustre to officially inspired Israeli propaganda which stressed the poor performance of Arab soldiers – Egyptian soldiers in particular.

Faced with this situation it is hardly surprising that Nasser came near to a nervous and physical collapse, and it was a gaunt and seemingly broken man who stood before the television cameras on 9th June 1967. 'We cannot hide from ourselves the fact that we have met with a grave setback in the last few days', he told his audience. The enemy plan to invade Syria had been the cause of the war, he said: 'it had been Egypt's duty not to accept this in silence'. The United States and the Soviet Union had both insisted on Egypt holding her fire. But the enemy had struck with a stronger blow than had been expected, showing that 'there were other forces behind him which came to settle their account with the Arab Nationalist Movement'. Nasser then declared that he was ready to assume entire responsibility for the 'setback'. He had. decided to give up all his official posts, and every political role, and become an ordinary citizen. He was, he said, handing over the Egyptian presidency to Vice-President Zachria Mohieddin. 'The forces of imperialism', he said, 'imagine that Abdul Nasser is their enemy, I want it to be clear that it is the entire Arab nation, and not Gamal Abdul Nasser'.

If the Egyptian leader's speech was intended to turn ignominy into personal triumph it certainly worked. As soon as they heard him announce his resignation people in Cairo began to pour out of their houses shouting for Nasser to stay. Sobbing men ran through the streets wailing 'Nasser, Nasser, don't leave us; we need you'. Thousands of people travelled into Cairo by car, bus and train to join the crowds which massed along the five-mile stretch of road from Nasser's house to the centre of Cairo. In Algeria mobs who had been shouting 'Lynch Nasser', suddenly changed their tune. From Damascus President Aref telephoned Cairo, urging Nasser to reconsider his decision; in the Lebanon President Helou is said to have broken down and wept when he heard that the Egyptian leader intended to resign. From Baghdad to Beirut Arab mobs swept into the streets to demonstrate for Nasser. Nearly all these demonstrations showed an ugly anti-American and anti-British bias; most of this was restricted to the shouting of slogans, but in Beirut a mob set fire to a Coca-Cola bottling plant on the grounds that it belonged to the 'US Imperialists'.

Mohieddin, Nasser's unaccepted nominee as his successor

If, as it now seems probable, a group of the senior Egyptian army officers were hatching a plot to depose Nasser, their chances of success were very small. Zacharia Mohieddin, whose policies were known to be pro-American, quickly announced that he would refuse to take over the presidency; the Egyptian Cabinet voted not to accept Nasser's resignation, and the Egyptian National Assembly did the same. As he had probably calculated all along, the Egyptian leader was able to '. . . bow to the voice of the people', to withdraw his resignation and to keep his job.

The other Arab political leaders also managed to survive in the immediate wake of the war. Like Nasser, King Hussein broadcast a public reckoning; unlike Nasser, however, he offered no alibis, made no excuses, and used no intemperate language to explain Jordan's defeat. Israel had won, he said, 'with overwhelming

strength . . . It is apparent that we have not yet learned well enough how to use the weapons of modern warfare.' Amid all the fantasies, delusions and confusion pervading the Arab world in the wake of the war, Hussein's voice was the most realistic. His country had fought the hardest and lost the most, but Hussein's personal reputation in Jordan and the Arab world was higher than ever. A cheering crowd in Amman converged on his Cadillac, picked it up and carried it five yards to demonstrate their adulation.

Stunned beyond belief, the Arab world appeared unable to comprehend the disaster which had overtaken it. It could no longer make war, but refused to make peace; it had lost its armies but was desperately determined not to lose its face. Throughout Islam, Moslem mullahs proclaimed American and British products unholy. 'Defeat exists only for those who admit it', said Cairo's semi-official newspaper *Al Gumhuria* a week after the war. 'We do not admit it.' Two weeks later another Cairo newspaper *Al Ahram* told its readers: 'The battle is still going on. Victory is ours.' In Damascus slogans newly painted on the walls of public buildings promised 'We shall destroy the enemy'. In both Beirut and Cairo the Arabs demanded that the name of the American University should be changed to Palestine University, and Algeria compiled a list of 'pro-Zionist' cinema stars, including Sophia Loren, Elizabeth

Popular feeling prevents Nasser's departure: here members of the National Assembly rise to demand that he should stay

Taylor and Harry Belafonte, and banned their films. Libyan mobs destroyed wine and liquor stores as symbols of US 'imperialism', and King Idris demanded that the United States abandon its Wheelers Air Force Base. Egypt and Syria closed their ports to American and British ships; Sudanese and Iraqi dock labourers refused to unload them. Behind these exercises in extended solipsism there was plenty of evidence of the realities of defeat, however. What was left of Jordan was swarming with refugees from the West Bank; Amman's normal population of 300,000 was swelled by at least 100,000 refugees, most of whom arrived destitute and hungry. Although schools, mosques and public buildings were hurriedly converted to provide sleeping accommodation, thousands of refugees had nowhere to go. They foraged for food, which rapidly became scarce and impossibly expensive. Hussein's government established two refugee camps, and other Arab nations sent emergency supplies of food, clothing and money. But these were barely sufficient and the problems of organization and distribution were exacerbated by inefficiency and national jealousies. For example Syria detained one Lebanese convoy for twelve hours before allowing it to proceed to Amman.

Cairo presented another grim picture of confusion, hysteria and dismay. Guards on the Nile bridges, government offices and important installations were doubled in the immediate aftermath of the war. Periodical air-raid alerts sent people scurrying for shelter, and the Egyptian Government issued a warning that watches, cigarette packets and fountain pens found in the streets were probably booby traps dropped by Israeli aircraft. In the absence of information regarding casualties and the extent of the debacle, Cairo's bazaars buzzed with rumours. Soldiers returning from Sinai blamed their misfortunes on their officers, and it was a long time before Egyptian Army officers could venture into the streets of Cairo in uniform without running the risk of being spat on.

In human and economic terms Jordan suffered more than Egypt from the war. Hussein's tough little Arab Legion fought hard, as is witnessed by the official casualty figures which listed 6,094 killed out of an estimated 50,000 soldiers who fought on the West Bank. How many men were wounded has never been disclosed, but 5,000 were said to be missing, although some of these turned up later among

Beirut airport after an Israeli retaliation raid, December 1968

the refugees who stole back across the river. Three-quarters of Jordan's tanks were lost in the fighting; so too were three-quarters of the army's guns, and the Royal Jordanian Air Force was left literally without planes. Territorially the cost was even greater. With the loss of the West Bank went most of Jordan's richest source of foreign-currency earnings, estimated at $35 million a year.

Egypt lost at least three-quarters of its air force, 800 of its 900 tanks – 300 of which were abandoned intact – and enormous quantities of other vehicles. The Israelis also claimed to have taken 400 field guns, fifty self-propelled guns, and thirty 155mm guns. The Russians mounted a massive airlift to replace some of these losses, but disenchantment with their Arab protegèes slowed this re-armament programme. The Arab defeat brought the Russians diplomatic and political loss of face, and with the Suez Canal out of action they faced frustrating logistic problems in building up the Soviet Navy as an 'instrument of diplomacy' in the Indian Ocean. Nasser had failed the Soviet Union and the Russians were not over-anxious to replace the entire $1 billion's worth of lost equipment – preferring to give the Egyptians the wherewithal for defence without making them capable of launching an attack on Israel.

With the occupation of Sinai, Egypt lost 20 per cent of its territory and its economy was in deplorable shape. Industrial output had slowed before the war started. By some estimates many new factories were operating at less than half capacity, owing to lack of spare parts and raw materials. Now, the four main sources of foreign exchange were either sick, dead, sunk, or in Israel. Because of the war tourism, which ordinarily brought in

$78 million a year, had dried up; the Suez Canal, which earned Egypt $260 million a year, was clogged with sunken ships; and the wells in Sinai, providing nearly 80 per cent of Egypt's oil production, were in Israeli hands. At the same time the cotton crop worth $300 million a year and mortgaged to the Soviet Union was threatened by the worst plague of cotton leafworms since the Second World War.

With the economy in a mess and the morale of the Egyptian army at an all time low, Nasser's pampered officer corps provided the scapegoats. Eleven generals were dismissed, including the army, navy and air force commanders and Field-Marshal Amer; hundreds of other officers were cashiered for desertion in the face of the enemy. The Russians, disgusted with the performance of the Egyptian Army and air force, insisted on a complete reorganization of the military in return for replacing the lost equipment.

Similar conditions were imposed on Syria which had lost six of its MiGs, 110 of its tanks and about half of the other armoured vehicles in its possession. President Atassi and the ruling Baathist party had been unmasked as paper tigers for championing total war and then limiting their offensive to shelling until the Israelis turned on them. So the Soviet Union was in no particular hurry to replace the lost equipment until the Syrian defence forces were purged. Syria had also lost some territory but as she had no oil or tourist industry she suffered much less economically than Egypt or Jordan. In effect the Israeli invasion of Syria united the Syrians and gave the Baathist government a new lease of life. Among all the belligerent Arab states Syria's attitude of 'No peace until Zionism ends', has been the most extreme.

The two brigades which Iraq sent to Jordan took heavy casualties in men and equipment, and the Israeli Air

King Feisal of Saudi Arabia

Force destroyed the seventeen Iraqi planes. But President Aref's moderate socialist regime emerged from the war without too many scars. Aref's troubles stemmed less from the war with Israel and his country's economy (80 per cent of Iraq's revenue is derived from oil), but from internal dissension caused by the Kurdish minority in the north and the Shiah Moslems in the south.

Apart from the two Hunter jets trespassing in Israeli air space on Tuesday 6th June, Lebanon did not clash with Israel. But it suffered badly in the war's aftermath. No one expected the Lebanese to fight, but their Christian-Moslem coalition government made belligerent noises, evicted the American ambassador and downgraded the American embassy to a legation. With the ambassador went the tourists which were the mainstay of Lebanon's economic life. Except for a few Arab diplomats, Beirut's luxury hotels were empty for a long time, and even when the tourists

Streams of refugees pour out of occupied territories into Jordan

started to drift back their numbers were greatly reduced, owing to the fact that 60 per cent of the pre-war tourists used the Lebanon as a stop-over on their way to Jerusalem, and access to the Holy City was now through Israel. Lebanon also suffered as a result of the activities of the Palestine Liberation Movement guerilla groups which insisted on operating against Israel from Lebanese territory. After the war the Palestine Liberation Organization was taken over by more militant groups, one of which, the Popular Front for the Liberation of Palestine (PFLP), hijacked an El Al plane. Israeli retaliation came swiftly, in the shape of a raid on Beirut international airport.

Saudi Arabia was untouched by the war; the troops it sent to Jordan did not fight and King Feisal stayed well away from the theatre of operations. As with Iraq, oil is the basis of Saudi Arabia's economy and this only suffered from the self-imposed Arab ban on export to the West. When the effect of this embargo, a loss estimated at $300,000 a day, began to be felt, it was lifted as being 'shortsighted and injurious to our overall economic position'. Meanwhile the King and his princes continued to send large donations to help buy new equipment for the shattered armies of the other Arab states.

In South Arabia, both the Yemen and the new People's Republic of South Yemen temporarily profited from the war, because their Arab patrons were forced to leave them alone. The Six Day War was mainly responsible for the withdrawal of Egypt from the Yemen although the civil war there continued briefly in a somewhat lower key.

Libya was not directly involved in the war, because its offer of troops was turned down by Nasser. But 77-year-old King Idris, who demonstrated support for the Arab cause by stopping oil production, telling the Americans to leave Wheeler Air Force Base, and the British to evacuate their army bases at Tobruk and Benghazi, was deposed by a pro-Nasser military coup in 1969.

Algeria, on the periphery of the Arab world, was barely affected by the war, since there was no involvement and the fighting was too remote. In the aftermath however, President Houari Boumedienne quickly made it clear he was anxious to replace Nasser as the new leader of the Arab left. Nasser had been closely associated with ex-President Ben Bella whom Boumedienne overthrew, and relations between Egypt and Algeria had never been warm or close since that time.

Moreover Boumedienne was keen to attract Soviet assistance for Algeria. When he flew to Moscow in the summer of 1967, the Algerian president became the first Arab leader to stage a summit visit to the Soviet Union since the Arab defeat. President Atassi of Syria, who also had an eye on the Arab leadership, quickly followed him. But neither man had sufficient popular following to threaten Nasser's leadership and by the end of 1969 Boumedienne appeared to have lost interest. Since then Algeria's attitude towards Arab affairs has become one of distant interest, approaching detachment.

Israel's gain and losses from the war have proved to be paradoxical. Prestige was her chief gain. But prestige had not been her war aim. The motives for her pre-emptive strike were not those proclaimed on the morning of 5th June, that is, a riposte to an Egyptian invasion. Nor was concern over Eilat more than symbolic, although lines of communications were important symbols. The Israelis' real hope was to compel their unrealistic neighbours to accept the Jewish State. And whatever the dimensions of this state might be they wanted security for it. (A complication was the wide difference of opinion as to the location of the frontiers of Israel, and some Israelis seem disposed to accept the newly extended territory as the reality they wished to secure.)

But Israel had won land as well as

Unstable and inadequate settlement: the refugees form a new and problematic community of canvas shelters and tin-roofed shacks

prestige from her six days of bloody battle. Much of this land, like Sinai, was an empty waste. But some of it was inhabited, and the conquest of people and property brings enormous obligations. 'We have conquered a dung-heap in order to win a pearl', said one Israeli soldier on the West Bank shortly after the cease-fire. 'We've got Jerusalem again – and we've got the refugee camps too.' After the war Israel found that she was responsible for the welfare of 1,330,000 hostile Arabs, more than a tenth of whom were impoverished refugees from the 1948 War of Independence. Those Arabs not only had to be fed and housed, but also policed and screened for saboteurs. In Gaza there were refugees who had emerged as commandos during the fighting and slipped back into their warren of tin-roofed shacks afterwards. Neither territory nor prestige could produce security. Before 1967 Israel's losses from border incursions had been irregular and small; they were certainly far less than the toll she had periodically inflicted on the Arabs in reprisal raids. Since 1967 Israel has had to keep a far larger number of her 230,000 army reservists in uniform and the number of Israeli casualties mounted with steady momentum, reaching in some months of 1969-70 around 100. By 1970 Israel was spending, in hard cash, more than $3 million a day on defence. For such an expenditure in blood and cash much of the land she had gained seemed to offer a bleak return.

Despite such difficulties the Israelis quickly succeeded to an astonishing degree in restoring normality. Following the pattern of the United States occupation of Japan they handed back authority to the mayors and city councils of Arab towns, and Arab officials were encouraged to restore communal services – water, electricity, sanitation – to towns and villages. New currency systems were devised and shops reopened. At the same time the Israelis were prepared to be ruthless when the situation-demanded toughness. The more frequent the attacks by the fedayeen the more the reprisals. Homes in which arms were found or reported to have been visited by Palestinian commandos were blown up; Arabs suspected of sabotage activities were summarily shipped off to prisoner-of-war camps. In Jerusalem Israeli soldiers evicted Arabs from what was once the Jewish quarter of the Old City; Arabs believed to be associated with the Palestine guerillas were seized and forced across the river into Jordan.

Inevitably these severities of military occupation brought victorious

Israel into closer and more bitter contact with the last and most important party to the war – the Palestinians. Before June 1967 most Palestinians had existed on the Arab side of the 1948 armistice line. 300,000 of them were enclosed in the Gaza Strip, many thousands more lived on the West Bank where their activities were supervised and curbed by Hussein's Arab Legion. Fedayeen activities had been on a relatively small scale up to the time of the crisis which provoked the war. But the defeat of the Arab armies gave a new impetus to the Palestine guerilla movement, Arab propaganda had promised certain victory over Israel, and in the humiliation of defeat the Palestinians came to realize, as never before, the bitter fact that for nearly twenty years they had been only a minor factor in the conflict. For the first time the Arab struggle against Israel began to get some sympathy in the west, and the Palestinians began to compare their cause with that of occupied Europe in the Second World War. Revered by the rest of the Arab world the guerilla attacks mounted from Jordan or Lebanon prompted Israeli reprisals – usually in the ratio of ten to one – which have scorched the east bank of the Jordan valley and threatened to turn southern Lebanon into a no-man's-land. More insidiously the glamour of the young men and young women in camouflage jackets and cheap canvas shoes threw into relief the failure of the expensive Arab armies.

Bibliography

The Six Days' War Israeli Ministry of Defence Official Account, Israel Press Tel Aviv 1967.

The Six Day War Lieutenant-Colonel A. Ayalon, Israel Army Spokesman's Office, Tel Aviv 1970.

The Six Day War Randolph S. Churchill and Winston S. Churchill, Heineman, London 1967.

The Third Arab-Israeli War Edgar O'Ballance, Faber & Faber, London 1972.

A Soldier's Diary, Sinai 1967 Lieutenant Yael Dayan, Weidenfeld & Nicolson, London 1968.

My 'War' With Israel Hussein of Jordan, William Morrow, New York 1969.

Nasser: A political Biography Robert Stephens, Allen Lane, The Penguin Press, London 1971.

The Tanks of Tammuz Shabtai Teveth, Weidenfeld & Nicolson, London 1969.

The Israeli Campaign 1967 Peter Young, William Kimber, London 1967.

My Country Abba Eban, Weidenfeld & Nicolson, London 1972.